ADVANCE PRAISE

"The traditional practice of management has hit a wall—it needs to change from 'boss to coach' to achieve really high-performance teams. It is harder than it looks—this culture transformation needs coaching itself—this book is a big step in the right direction."

—JIM CLIFTON, CHAIRMAN AND CEO
OF THE GALLUP ORGANIZATION

"TLC—Talent, Leadership & Culture is the new superfuel driving company growth, innovation and performance. My good friend Joe brilliantly shares proven strategies that improve performance and lives—a must read."

—GREG PRYOR, SVP, PEOPLE AND PERFORMANCE
EVANGELIST AT WORKDAY (#4 ON FORTUNE'S
LIST OF 100 BEST COMPANIES TO WORK FOR)

"Pick up the Gum Wrapper is a fantastic tool for team development. Not only does it help you identify the individual strengths within your team, you are also able to harness those strengths and take your team to the next level. Joe's insight shines through in this book, he has worked with our team for years, and his guidance has elevated our performance and created an atmosphere where people utilize their strengths on a daily basis."

—ERIC GELLY, PRESIDENT OF CUNA STRATEGIC SERVICES

"As a first-year CEO with a new executive team, we engaged Joe to assist in the development of that team and our organization's culture. Identifying each of our strengths, similarities, and differences has helped build a cohesive team, all moving in the same direction, all desiring to Pick Up the Gum Wrapper. The chapter on setting and living the organization's Behavioral Expectations was eye opening. Joe's expertise in leadership development is incredible, and his presentation style is captivating. The book reinforces the concepts he teaches and provides excellent examples and tools that are practical."

—BRET H. KREVOLIN, PRESIDENT/CEO,
UTILITIES EMPLOYEES CREDIT UNION

"Joe has been our culture champion for over a decade. During this time, we have consistently been named 'Best Places to Work' and measured the highest levels of employee engagement. With Joe, we have the right people in the right positions! This book is a must-read if you strive to pick up the gum wrapper at work and beyond."

—MARK MERRILL, CHAIRMAN AND CEO,
OLD DOMINION NATIONAL BANK

"Joe is an expert on leadership development and helping you utilize your strengths to be more of an effective leader. He has been our leadership consultant for the past three years—we have seen a huge improvement in how we interact as a leadership team and the overall culture of the organization."

—MARIA A. LAVELLE, CEO, PHEPLE FCU

"It is not often that you get the opportunity to meet someone who has the ability to see into your soul. Joe Bertotto is a legend unto his own and has provided years of both personal and professional guidance, not only to myself, but to my co-workers and credit union professionals in our industry.

"Despite our many initial obstacles, Destinations CU has definitely found its direction by utilizing the goals and implementing the timelines Joe has set in measuring our continued progress. Pick Up the Gum Wrapper embodies all of these sentiments, and reinforces how fortunate I've been to become a better leader by crossing paths with Mr. Bertotto!"

—BRIAN J. VITTEK, PRESIDENT/CEO OF
DESTINATIONS CREDIT UNION

"Joe teaches us how to make companies great by bringing out the greatness in our employees and ourselves. If you want a team where everyone would Pick up the Gum Wrapper, read on."

—LAWRENCE M. KLUGER, PRESIDENT AND
CEO, RHODES DEVELOPMENT GROUP

PICK UP THE GUM WRAPPER

PICK UP THE GUM WRAPPER

HOW TO CREATE A WORKPLACE
THAT INCREASES PERFORMANCE
WHILE IMPROVING LIVES

JOE BERTOTTO

LIONCREST
PUBLISHING

PICK UP THE GUM WRAPPER
How to Create a Workplace That Increases
Performance While Improving Lives

ISBN   978-1-5445-0591-6 *Paperback*
            978-1-5445-0590-9 *Ebook*

For Judy, the love of my life, and the cutest, most clever person I know. For Alex, my main man, a strategic thinker with a quick wit who overcomes challenges whether it's a mountain or a wave and a remarkable person who sparked this book. For Melanie, my little peach, equal parts homebody and adventurer, a future champion of animals who's happy floating in the water or sliding eighty miles an hour down ice tracks.

CONTENTS

INTRODUCTION

I couldn't believe it as I listened to a group of young friends talk with great enthusiasm about the day when they could leave their jobs to live the good life. Twenty and thirty-somethings talking about retiring? Wow! What a shame to dislike what you do so much that you would wish your day, week, year—well—basically, wish your life away!

Sadly, so many people feel this way. However, your work **can** provide the opposite experience. A place where your contributions are valued and celebrated. A place where you have a strong sense of affiliation with your colleagues as you strive to accomplish great things for customers and one another. A sense of purpose. A place where you are not only accepted for who you are but also encouraged and supported as you grow. A place where you're doing more of the work you're good at and enjoy. Think of the personal satisfaction that comes when **you** reshape the work experience. If they had a place like that, those young friends of mine would be eternally grateful.

It really can be like that. What companies need are leaders who also want that same supportive environment and are courageous enough to do what it takes to install the right elements. That's what these pages offer. **I've made this a hybrid guidebook/workbook of sorts with tips and tools you can readily apply.** When I read a business book—and I've read a lot of them—the ones I find most useful are the books that give me specific practices I can begin to implement. That's what I've provided for you here. From agendas to activities, there are tools you can begin to use immediately after you read them. You may have to refine them to fit your style. I hope you'll share them with others. We all have a responsibility to make our workplaces great.

YOU can be that person who makes the shift happen in your workplace. Think about that: you can be someone who can change the lives of others. You can be the person who makes work enjoyable for yourself and others. It's not easy, and there aren't shortcuts, but the energy you feel will propel you through and around the inevitable obstacles. The other thing that will energize you like the thrust of a rocket booster is the business results of this workplace improvement. I'll provide specific examples as these pages unfold.

This process—the process of building a culture of people who pick up the gum wrappers—works. I've used it to help companies become Best Places to Work, increase their employee engagement to numbers that almost double the national average and, most of all, to have more people feeling good about walking through the door to their workplace each day rather than thinking about how soon they can walk back *out* that door.

The bottom line is that all of this leads to better performance. It's no mystery that when we're enthused about something, we tend to work harder at it while enjoying it more. The mystery has always been how to make the overall experience of work one that creates and sustains that enthusiasm. I'd like to think my contribution helps solve that mystery.

From a personal standpoint, my passion is helping others get to the same place. I live and breathe leadership and culture, so much so that I think I've read the majority of books published on these subjects over the past few decades. I even do my own version of book reports.

But I wasn't always this way, as you'll learn. I experienced the Sunday night dreads and lottery wishes just like many of you, and that's what drives me. I know it can be different. When I found the role that matched my natural talents and worked for leaders who built trusting relationships and invested in me, my life became much better—not just my work life, but my whole life.

Keep making a positive impact!

Joe B

CHAPTER 1

WHY MAKE THE EFFORT?

"Are you excited?" That was the question my dad asked me as we got out of the car and walked toward Connie Mack Stadium. The answer was obvious. I loved baseball, and I was getting my first chance to see my favorite Philadelphia Phillies player Richie (later called Dick) Allen in person. I was so excited I couldn't contain myself. I was only eight years old, but I think my dad was struggling to keep pace with me. I was moving as fast as I could to get to the turnstiles. I didn't want to miss one pitch. I got rewarded, too, when my boyhood hero hit one out of the park early in the game. After the game, I was still so excited that I couldn't wait to get home to tell my mom all about it and hang the Phillies pennant my dad bought me on my bedroom wall.

Are you that excited to go to work? It's unrealistic to replicate the level of excitement I felt as a little boy going to my first baseball game, but that doesn't mean you can't have a spring in your step as you walk through the doors of your office. **If you're like the majority of the working population, the steps you take to the office on most days are hesitant ones filled with angst or apathy.** It shouldn't be like that. Work should be a place that fosters craftsmanship, self-expression, and camaraderie. A place where you're proud to belong. A place where you have friendships as you work toward meaningful goals. A place that gives you purpose. One where tasks are opportunities to leverage the best you have to offer, not chores that numb your mind.

This description isn't a fairy tale; both in my role as chief culture officer within my organization and as a consultant to other companies looking to transform their culture, I've seen it happen time and time again—but it isn't a quick or easy process. It takes consistent effort and intentionality. But when you have success, no one on the team goes to bed on Sunday night with a feeling of dread for the workweek ahead. The Monday morning walk toward the office isn't like walking the plank. Heading to a meeting, if someone sees a gum wrapper on the floor, they pick it up. They're proud to keep the office presentable and don't see how a colleague could be so careless. That's how invested they are in their work and their organization.

THREE KINDS OF EMPLOYEES

The analogy of the gum wrapper illustrates the three kinds of employees at organizations today: some pick up discarded gum wrappers, others see them but walk by, and a few contribute to the negative work environment by throwing them down in the first place. Let's take a closer look.

1. **Employees Who Pick Up the Gum Wrappers.** These employees continuously give their best effort on projects, volunteer within the company and community, and take initiative. They solicit customers even outside of work hours, and they help recruit team members they feel will fit well within the organization. They ask their teammates, fellow employees, and boss, "Does anybody need help? Is there anything I can do?" Research shows only 34 percent of employees fall into this category.[1] That's not a very high percentage. Think about the performance of a work team where that number doubled!

2. **Employees Who Leave the Gum Wrappers on the Floor.** These employees are often mostly committed to their job, but not enough to give it their discretionary effort on a regular basis. They will show up on time and do a good job within their role, but initiative

---

1   Gallup. "Employee Engagement on the Rise in the U.S." Gallup.com. August 26, 2018. Accessed April 15, 2019. https://news.gallup.com/poll/241649/employee-engagement-rise. aspx.

is not something they prioritize. You'll hear them say, "I do my job and go home. It's not my responsibility to pick up anything extra." That same data shows 53 percent of employees see themselves in this category. Many of those people are looking for a reason to pick up the gum wrapper. Creating the right environment by meeting their needs will do the trick.

3. **Employees Who Drop the Gum Wrappers.** These employees are miserable at work, and their discontent isn't exactly a secret in the office. While those who walk by the gum wrappers may take initiative on occasion, those who throw them down will not. They'll say, "I can't stand it here. I'm here because I have to be." These employees are typically few in number, around 13 percent according to Gallup's most recent data, but they poison the well and drag everyone's morale and performance down. They can make even the best employee's lives glum.

Odds are, your organization has all three types of employees; that's typical. Just because a team member leaves the gum wrapper today doesn't mean they won't pick it up tomorrow. **While some who drop the gum wrappers might be CAVE dwellers—that is, they're Consistently Against Virtually Everything—deep down, some of them might just be looking for a reason to be the person who picks them up someday.** Most people don't want to *have* to go to work; they want to *get* to go to work. Establishing an environment where everyone feels valued and inspired will create a team of collaborative, motivated, and productive employees—and that's what will drive your organization forward.

BUILDING A PRODUCTIVE CULTURE

You want your team to pick up the gum wrappers. You want them to do their job well and enjoy their time at work. This not only boosts their levels of productivity—thereby bolstering the company's success—but it also speaks to a basic part of our humanity: we all want to be fulfilled and happy at work. You can help spearhead this culture shift by being a servant leader, recognizing that you set the tone within your organization and working to help improve the lives of those who work *with*—not *for*—you. Culture is driven by the relationships we have at work. It can be difficult to get people to come together day after day in a supportive way. There are nuances and pressures. People with minds of their own and people with annoying idiosyncrasies. Accepting each person for who they are can feel impossible at times. But we can do it and you can be the catalyst.

As Sam Houston, the only American to be elected governor in two different states, said, "A leader is someone who helps improve the lives of other people or improve the system they live under." That's the power of leadership.

There are three components to building a productive culture and propelling your organization forward:

+ Learning, appreciating, and leveraging each employee's uniqueness
+ Identifying Behavioral Expectations
+ Defining leadership practices that are designed to build a workplace culture rooted in high care, high performance, and high accountability.

There are subtleties to each component, and the path through the process isn't linear. It takes time and dedication to create a workplace in which teams can thrive. Moving through these components takes effort. After more than thirty years of doing this work, I've seen what makes a difference in an organization, and I've seen how profound that difference is. At the end of the day, we're all trying to do our best work. **No one is coming into the office asking himself, "How can I screw up today?"** To be a good leader and help your team rise to their fullest potential, sometimes you need to take the uncommon approach. While there can be uncertainty in not playing it like everyone else, your results can also be unlike everyone else's.

COMPONENT 1: LEARN ABOUT EMPLOYEE UNIQUENESS WITH CLIFTONSTRENGTHS®

To me, there aren't many *universal* laws of human dynamics, but here is one that holds true: people want to be accepted and appreciated for who they are. You know how you feel when someone accepts you without judgment. You don't have to waste time pretending to be someone you aren't. As a leader, instead of trying to change people to fit a role or a way of working, focus on working within the natural makeup of those people to bring out their best. **Spend your energy capitalizing on what's already there.** It's easier for you and the members of your team. That's what understanding employee uniqueness is about. One leader recently told me he rarely looked at the natural gifts of his employees. Didn't really give it much thought. He appreciated them but was more concerned with the pressure of achieving the necessary results. Once he recognized these gifts, he began to approach them differently. He became humbled by the awesome talent each one brought to the team. He began to notice when they enjoyed a task and when they performed another task well enough but looked drained. He began to adjust the way he distributed work ever so slightly based on which member of the team enjoyed the work and was good at it. Ultimately, a whole new world opened up to him, as already good relationships became even stronger and overall performance boosted. The same outcome will be true for you.

The data supports what this leader found: playing to the strengths of each team member can result in profitability gains of as much as 14 percent.[2]

Just to be clear, accepting people for who they are doesn't give someone who is behaving badly the right to continue acting like that or say, "That's just who I am, so live with it." As we'll discuss later, unproductive behavior should never be tolerated. If it is tolerated, it will rapidly destroy what you're trying to create.

I use a digital assessment tool from Gallup® called the CliftonStrengths® Assessment to help people see what makes them special. Participants answer questions about themselves, and the tool provides insight into their top talents and strengths in a highly personalized way. (I'll cover CliftonStrengths in depth in Chapter Two. You'll also see I have placed brackets around the short theme definitions of these talents as we discuss them, so you can refer to them easily.) In short, CliftonStrengths shows us how we're unique, what we're both good at *and* enjoy, as well as where we might be undermining our own success. It's wildly effective; over 20,000,000 people have taken the assessment to date, and the book—*StrengthsFinder 2.0*—is a number one selling nonfiction book on Amazon.

---

2   Gallup. "7 Ways to Use CliftonStrengths to Improve Your Employee Experience Strategy." Gallup.com. October 22, 2018. Accessed April 15, 2019. https://www.gallup.com/workplace/243791/ways-cliftonstrengths-improve-employee-experience-strategy.aspx.

Self-awareness is the gateway to personal mastery. As a leader, if you know the individuals on your team and how they are likely to act and react to situations, you can leverage that information to help them be happier and perform better. This is critical because according to research from Gallup, people who get to use their strengths every day at work report being six times more engaged in their jobs. They're also three times more likely to report a higher quality of life.

COMPONENT 2: IDENTIFY COMPANY BEHAVIORAL EXPECTATIONS

The CliftonStrengths Assessment shows us how we're different. Creating Behavioral Expectations, on the other hand—usually labeled "core values" that form the base of how employees act in an organization—helps us think about how we're the same, giving a sense of predictability to interactions that leads to trust. I write "core values" in quotes because, in many organizations, their "core values" are highly general, and they're rarely used in conjunction with accountability or action. Behavioral Expectations are different.

Behavioral Expectations are the kinds of commitments you make about how you're going to work as a community of people. (I'll cover Behavioral Expectations in depth in Chapter Three.) They go beyond givens like "respect" and "honesty." Crafting targeted, actionable Behavioral Expectations—and, more importantly, living and reinforcing them—is a key to creating an environment where interactions are consistent. As leaders and as employees, we've all had to address awkward or negative interpersonal situations. Behavioral Expectations set the precedent for how people are treated. No guessing games. As an example, one organization had difficulty with follow-through; it was spotty and in reality depended on who was expected to follow through as to whether or not something got done. One of the Behavioral Expectations we developed was *"Yes Means Yes."* That means if you say yes, honor your commitment. If you can't do it as or when requested, then say no or negotiate the deliverable before you say yes. The senior leadership team agreed that the lack of follow-through was slowly fracturing the company and killing performance. They also agreed to correct the problem by ensuring that they kept their promises to one another. With a lot of attention, the problem improved. Some of that attention came in the form of discussing when the expectation everyone agreed to wasn't met. Feeling their colleagues were reliable built trust among the team. Another form of the attention was leaders looking for root causes for the lack of follow-through in conflicting processes and competing demands—which takes us to the third element of our process.

COMPONENT 3: BUILD DEFINED LEADERSHIP PRACTICES

Leaders are culture carriers; what the leader pays attention to is what team members pay attention to. I think we can all agree we'd prefer to stay away from the disastrous disconnect when leaders feel they're above or immune to following standards to which they hold others.

As leaders, we have the opportunity to accept people for who they are, focus on and leverage their strengths, and reinforce and live the Behavioral Expectations of the company. Now, we don't have to do everything—as CliftonStrengths shows us, not everyone excels at the same things. By better understanding our team and the individuals on it, however, we can leverage the right tools and the right people to drive engagement and boost performance. Reaching this point, though, starts by defining leadership practices that create and boost the culture we aim to build. I'll discuss how to do this in depth when we discuss Component 3, as I share the following leadership practices that you can use to help create a team that is more productive, more collaborative, and more energized. I'll also provide tools, exercises, and strategies related to these leadership practices you can use to improve the health of your organization.

- **Make Meaning.** It's no secret that you can excel at tasks you don't truly enjoy. You do them because you have to. Part of a leader's job is to stop that cycle and help people discover what meaningful work looks like to them. That process can involve asking important questions: "Why do you get up in the morning?" "Why do you come to work?" "What do you love about this job, and what don't you love?" You'll also ask, "How can you make it better for yourself?" and—most importantly from a leadership perspective—"How can I help make it better for you?"

+ **Manage to Outcomes.** The CliftonStrengths Assessment shows it's incredibly rare for two employees to have the exact same Strengths profile. It also shows we have different preferences and personality traits that contribute not only to what we like to do but how we do it. When you manage to outcomes, you have the opportunity to honor each team member not only for their talents but also for the unique ways in which they conduct their work. The key is to set expectations and offer coaching and support, yet be able to confidently say, "We agreed to a goal, so get there in whatever way is comfortable for you." It's easy to become overzealous with a do-it-this-way approach, but resisting that urge empowers people.

+ **Act with Benevolence.** Leaders who act with benevolence build trust and inspire people. Benevolence is about putting the interests of your team members equal to your own. There are many ways to do this. Whether it's asking for input and acting on it or working the day before a holiday so a member of your team can have off for a four-day weekend, consistently putting the interests of others before your own bonds people like nothing else.

- **Celebrate Individuals.** There are few laws of human dynamics that are universal, but one that I believe says that everyone likes to feel accepted and appreciated for who they are. The practical implication is that the way to show acceptance and appreciation is different for everyone. Remember, CliftonStrengths shows us how different we are, and that includes our interpretations of what makes appreciation significant. Not everyone likes to be recognized publicly, while someone else may thrive on it. **For recognition to be meaningful, it must be personalized to the person receiving it.** Understanding what is cherished by each person is essential to bringing out the best in her.

- **Work toward the Greater Good.** It can be easy to fixate only on responsibilities specifically assigned to us. We prioritize our own to-do lists, and, even if another's tasks are at cross-purposes to ours, we don't pay all that much attention. It's ironic that we all work for the same company but usually care primarily about our own results. Sometimes, we can push for our own success to the detriment of our employer. That typically suboptimizes overall company performance and snuffs out cross-functional teamwork.

While that mentality is usually incented, you can break the cycle. **You can be a catalyst for cohesion by always focusing on what's best for your entire organization.**

YOU WANT TO DO YOUR BEST—THAT'S WHY YOU'RE READING THIS BOOK

Creating a culture where team members pick up the gum wrapper does take effort, but the results are worth the investment. Take a minute and imagine an organization where the overwhelming majority of people are consistently offering to help one another, volunteering, and taking initiative for the success of the company. They'll likely be willing to work extra if they need to, and they're always looking to recruit new customers and new employees they feel might be a good fit.

Now, compare that culture to that of the average workplace, where many people are unhappy and often unwilling to volunteer for any project outside their respective job descriptions. There is complaining, negative water cooler talk, and service is an afterthought.

The company with the first culture has found the key that unlocks the door to a great workplace. That's not to say bits and pieces of the second company culture might not creep in now and then, but those instances are rare and addressed quickly based on ingrained practices and expectations. I've seen it happen: companies I've worked for and with have won Best Place to Work contests. One has *almost doubled* the national average of engaged employees—the figure that effectively measures how many employees will pick up the gum wrapper. Gallup was the first to coin the term "engagement" to describe employees who are enthused about their work and enthusiastic about their workplace. Essentially engagement is where performance and attitude intersect. Engaged employees pick up the gum wrapper and give their best consistently so these companies are also high performing financially. Many boast superior profitability. That's really the end result of doing this work on culture. Employees with great attitudes, positioned to do the work they are good at and enjoy, make the company successful on a variety of key performance metrics. In this book, I'll share how you can get there.

Next, let's look at a few overarching truths about building a great workplace. From there, we'll study each of the three components to creating a positive and productive culture. First, we'll review how to learn, appreciate, and leverage each employee's unique gifts using the CliftonStrengths Assessment—a tool built on decades of research on excellence. Second, we'll detail how to create Behavioral Expectations, the foundation of team interactions. Finally, we'll discuss the effective leadership practices that make everything else work. Institutional-izing these three components requires effort. This isn't quick or easy, but the payoff of better performance and greater happiness is worth the energy. Consider it a few giant steps for you, and one giant leap for your team!

CHAPTER 2

OVERARCHING PRINCIPLES FOR CREATING CULTURE

In one organization I worked for, the leadership was fractured. Most employees worried about their own individual goals, but they didn't give much thought to the greater good. Interpersonal relationships weren't terrible, but they weren't solid either. Instead of talking through conflicts, employees went directly to managers, missing opportunities to better understand one another and resolve issues. As a result, these conflicts escalated because people felt hurt and hung out to dry. This company operated like many organizations operate: the company was performing well on the outside while inside cohesion and engagement were low. For the most part, team members did what they had to do because they had to do it—nothing more. You might be thinking: if the company is performing well on the outside, does it really matter what's happening inside? According to Gallup, companies with highly engaged workforces outperformed their peers by 147 percent in earnings per share. It matters. And it matters to the people who come to work every day and their families.[3]

Armed with this knowledge, I set out to help this particular organization thrive. The following process happened over a long period of time, but it did get us to the finish line. First, because people who manage others set the tone when it comes to culture, I decided to start by creating unity within the senior leadership team. I had the leaders take the CliftonStrengths Assessment to increase their self-awareness and to help them better understand one another. Most of the time, no one comes to work to screw up or make their colleagues' lives miserable. Most reasonable people try to do their best and get along with others every day. So I reminded these leaders to give the benefit of the doubt among themselves and with everyone in the company.

With ongoing intentional collaboration with the senior team, leaders learned to reframe the discontent in the

---

3   Gallup. "Managers Account for 70% of Variance in Employee Engagement." Gallup.com. April 21, 2015. Accessed May 02, 2018. http://news.gallup.com/businessjournal/182792/managers-account-variance-employee-engagement.aspx.

office as stemming from misunderstandings instead of rushing to blame. They presumed innocence and focused on building relationships based on talents and strengths, following the advice of Ralph Waldo Emerson, who said, "What you do speaks so loudly that I cannot hear what you say." These leaders emulated and reinforced the dynamic they wanted to create within the organization, and it worked. As barriers began to melt between them, employees began to communicate more. As they formed better relationships internally, their team members were able to provide more effective and fluid service to one another and their customers. This cascading effect is the natural benefit when leaders understand their influence in creating the company's culture.

LEVERAGING INFLUENCE TO CREATE UNITY

I started with the senior leadership team because they are the tone-setters for the organization. Their styles and attitudes permeate through the company, affecting not only how people at all levels perform but how committed they are to the company and their coworkers. **A key question each senior leader should ask herself is, "What kind of organization are we trying to create, and how can we create it in a way that drives unity?"**

Unity is critical in organizations, because when everyone comes together and pulls in the same direction, incredible progress can be made. If people are tugging in different directions, it's difficult to move forward. Unity starts with those at the top, because, as research from Gallup shows, leaders (at any level) have an average of 76 percent of the influence in defining their team's engagement. That means the rest of the team has a combined 24 percent—which shouldn't be discounted, as everyone has a hand in creating culture.[4] Leaders, though, have the lion's share of influence in the creation and maintenance of a single culture. This statistic is telling because most organizations have as many subcultures as they do managers. Diligently paying attention to how leaders lead at every level helps to minimize these differences establishing one overarching culture.

IT'S ABOUT THE TEAM

As leaders, we are the glue that holds company culture together by creating a positive workplace, fostering development, nurturing engagement, and building bridges across the company. Building bridges is especially important because it is the most underused element of leadership.

Teams and managers can become so focused on their

---

4   Gallup. "Managers Account for 70% of Variance in Employee Engagement." Gallup.com. April 21, 2015. Accessed May 02, 2018. http://news.gallup.com/businessjournal/182792/managers-account-variance-employee-engagement.aspx.

own to-do lists that they neglect to consider how their work interfaces with that of their colleagues or affects the big-picture mission of the company. The reality is that no team works in a vacuum. Each person, and each department, is interdependent in some way or another. Sales cannot succeed without marketing. Marketing cannot succeed without IT. IT cannot succeed without finance. The sooner you can inspire your team to understand that everyone needs to work together, not in silos, the more efficient the organization can be.

Another way to think of this dynamic is to consider a sports jersey; there's the team logo on the front and the athlete's name on the back. If all of the athletes on the team play for the logo, the team will usually perform at a higher level than if they play with only concern for their own stats. The success of the logo on the front is the priority. This doesn't mean everyone agrees on everything or is quick to acquiesce, but it does mean decisions are made based on what is best for the collective. Counterintuitively, this mentality will ultimately result in individual success because people begin to rely on one another and support one another to reach greater heights.

Here is an example of how all of this comes together like a well-planned Thanksgiving dinner. Eric[5] was the manager of a credit union and a believer in the process

5   Names have been changed throughout this book.

I advocate. He had full-time tellers stationed inside the branch to assist customers (referred to as members in the credit union industry). This particular branch had only about one hundred members per day come in to transact business, leaving quite a bit of downtime for the tellers. Many of the tellers filled the time by reading books, surfing the internet, or chatting with one another, but Eric wanted to see if he could leverage their natural gifts to improve the credit union's performance and help bring more meaning to their workdays. He asked each teller what else she enjoyed doing and looked for ways to incorporate her answers into her daily responsibilities.

Eric never thought, "You're just a teller, so this is all you're required to do or are capable of." Instead, he chose a different path. One that leveraged strengths, enhanced contributions to create meaning and supported the entire credit union, not just one team. He thought, "You have so many amazing gifts. How can I help you use those better during your time here in a way that benefits us all and makes you feel great about your contribution to the organization?" Eric discovered one of his tellers was interested in marketing, so he put her in touch with the marketing team to see if she could be the merchandising champion for the branch. Another teller enjoyed researching, and she was thrilled when Eric asked her to help use her talents to compile information for another manager's weekly presentations. All of this added support across the credit union and contributed to greater year-end profitability. Ultimately, Eric looked beyond job descriptions because he understood something incredibly important: **people are bigger than their jobs.**

LEADERS ARE HUMAN, TOO

It's Eric's job to spearhead a culture that builds bridges, fosters unity, and promotes strength-based high performance—and he did that. But he did that by playing to his strengths and being aware of his weaknesses. As the leader, you don't need to be the person who has to do everything. Somewhere along the way leaders were epitomized as the people who had to be all knowing and all doing. **The leader needing to have super-human powers is a pervasive fallacy.** That's an impossible mountain to climb. It's also unfair and completely unrealistic.

In an environment where everyone's strengths and weaknesses are known, you can leverage the right people who have the talents you don't. Obviously, there are tasks that only you as the leader can perform, but when you honestly assess those, they're few in number. Formally disciplining and rating performance are the obvious ones. Depending on your style and the composition of the team, there may be a few other ones (arbitrating disagreements that the team can't solve or making the final decision on a project or assignment). But, believe me, **most of the must-dos of a leader are self-imposed.** That said, there are legitimate ways to fill skills gaps for the benefit of the team and the organization. It's a conscious form of delegation and also a way to develop others.

I'll share precisely how to do this when we discuss Effective Leadership Practices in Component 3, but let me give you an example of what this looks like. Say you're a manager who's exceptionally results-driven. You get satisfaction out of checking assignments off your list. You know you often forget to recognize team members when they do a great job. It's not that you intentionally overlook their accomplishment; you're just so goal oriented that you move onto the next item on your list. If you recognize this about yourself and admit it to your team, you can ask for help. Of course, many of them probably know this about you anyway, but since you've come clean and made yourself vulnerable, you can seek their support by tapping the team member who loves to cheer people on for their accomplishments. This person can be your surrogate by carrying the recognition banner for the team and by gently nudging you when acknowledgment is warranted. This way, everyone wins. You're relieved that you won't unintentionally miss the next opportunity to praise a deserving teammate, the employee helping you gets to spend time doing something they enjoy and are good at, and members of the team are being complimented for their good work. The other significant outcome of this approach is your candor about what you don't do well, and asking for help increases the level of trust within the team. **Vulnerability tightens the bonds of camaraderie, making people more human among their colleagues.**

This form of conscious delegation is critical, especially when you consider how busy managers are. Very few of us only manage people; there is work of our own to do and goals of our own to meet. This is the top reason the people part of the role can fall to the side. Ignoring the team eventually results in lagging productivity and minimized camaraderie. A focus on the team should be the primary responsibility of our role as managers. **When people are second to our individual work, our culture, and the benefits a positive one brings, will suffer.**

For example, I once started working with an organization and was surprised to learn their long-standing senior leadership team had *never held a team meeting.* Each leader was completing his individual work and occasionally meeting with the team who reported to him. The uber-busy CEO felt like she didn't have time for team meetings, there was too much to be done. The CEO would have impromptu meetings with each member of the leadership team, but those meetings were generally task- or project-focused. As a result, no one except the

CEO had a crystal-clear picture of how the organization was meeting its strategic goals. Members of the leadership team were accomplishing daily tasks—sometimes, even duplicating daily tasks without knowing it—but the work of running the business was left to the CEO alone. This suboptimized overall performance of the credit union, as collaboration was severely limited. Since the team never met together, communication was spotty, as the CEO would tell some things to some leaders but not others. This caused confusion, which led to rumors and misunderstanding.

To fix these issues, I recommended the senior leadership team meet weekly. In addition, each meeting had to have an agenda with deliverables—what needed to be done by when and by whom—and the person in charge of creating that agenda changed each week. The meeting's leader solicited agenda items from all members of the team. This ensured everyone was involved in constructing the content. Rotating who facilitated the meeting lessened the burden on the already overworked CEO and gave each leader an opportunity to increase his influence with his peers. (Later, I'll offer tools for meeting agendas and give you tips on how to conduct those meetings so they're as productive as can be.)

This practice—combined with learning one another's strengths via the CliftonStrengths Assessment and creating Behavioral Expectations—helped build the communication and trust that ultimately led to greater cohesion, performance, and exceeding the goals in the strategic plans.

START WITH A PROVEN MINDSET

As we walk through this process of creating a culture that makes employees want to pick up the gum wrappers, you'll want to have a mindset that emphasizes consistency, intentionality, and alignment. These three elements are the underpinnings you need to build the culture you want.

CONSISTENCY

To develop an enduring culture, you need to resist the urge to deviate from the plan, like creating different Behavioral Expectations to solve an immediate problem or introducing new assessments or leadership practices that are "fresh." This can be hard, because we can often think, "I'm repeating myself, so I've got to come up with something new," or, "This is getting stale. I've got to reenergize everyone." In reality, we're best served staying the course when it comes to culture because a consistent approach provides clarity, which leads to a greater understanding. With a greater understanding of what we're trying to create, it is more likely that the culture will be lived and, over time, institutionalized. Consistency builds predictability and, ultimately, trust.

This isn't to say that we shouldn't be innovative in other aspects of the business. We must be to advance in a world that is ever changing. We just want to limit that innovation to our products and services—not our culture. When we jump at the newest management idea or go online to find another assessment, it short-circuits the goal of an enduring culture and confuses people on the team. I've witnessed this kind of action time and again. While it's well-meaning, it's ill-advised. The random introduction of new things into the culture diminishes long-term effectiveness because it serves as a distraction to the core principles you need to become second nature to people. **Don't be tempted by the novel; keep the essential elements consistent.**

INTENTIONALITY

We must be intentional about how we manage people's strengths and how we model and reinforce the Behavioral Expectations. We've got to be intentional, too, in our leadership style and the way we perform the practices. To go into this process haphazardly or half-heartedly won't work. Gum wrappers will litter the hallways. We've got to be deliberate and purposeful. That means thinking about leveraging one person's strengths to help a colleague or following through on a commitment made to a member of our team when other, seemingly more pressing and important, actions need to be taken.

Here's an example of intentionality in action: a leader I worked with realized that a member of his team was just not suited for the role she was in based on her natural talents. The employee was an ambassador for the Behavioral Expectations of the company and an excellent fit in the culture. The leader also recognized this about her, so the leader worked directly with the employee and the Chief of Human Resources to create a position that would more easily leverage the natural gifts of the employee. It would have been easier for the already busy leader not to go through the effort and corporate rigmarole to do this and just terminate the underperforming employee, but he knew that would not be the right approach given the culture he was trying to uphold. It also sent a clear message to the rest of the team about working at a company that cares for everyone and leverages the best in each employee. **Intentionality is all about acting purposefully congruent with the culture you're trying to create.**

ALIGNMENT

Alignment means ensuring that all people processes match the culture we're trying to create. Alignment is a product of consistency and intentionality; it is hard to reach alignment without those in place. As we build a positive and productive culture, we may start to see misalignment between some business procedures and the new culture. When that occurs, we need to adjust procedures so they follow the new, improved culture. Otherwise, the effort to build a magical workplace rings hollow. Think about any company that claims people are their greatest asset, yet when one of those valued assets maxes out their salary range, the person is no longer eligible for a merit increase. Everyone will point to that as an example of why people are not that company's greatest asset. Mass cynicism will occur and resistance to a culture build will follow. Conversely, when procedures support the culture, employees are not confused or frustrated because procedures that impact them match the expectations of the culture. This alignment opens the door wide for everyone to willingly join in the culture build.

Here is an example of one company creating alignment by revamping a procedure to match the culture: the company listed as one of their Behavioral Expectations *Employees First,* and many actions they took aligned with this, including a weeklong employee appreciation celebration. One procedure that didn't match up was the mileage reimbursement for business travel. When an employee of this company drove from one office to another using their personal vehicle, they were reimbursed at a rate several cents below the governmental guideline. All organizations I've worked with and for reimburse employees at the government rate. Originally done by someone in the finance department as a temporary cost-saving measure, the policy remained in place well after it should have expired. When this was brought to the attention of the CEO, he immediately revised the policy in favor of the employees and at a significant cost to the company.

BE THE EXAMPLE FOR ALL TO FOLLOW

The biggest determinant in an employee picking up the gum wrapper is watching their leader pick up the gum wrappers. If we want to inspire elite performance in our team, we've got to show the way. At one bank I worked with, there was a nuisance tree limb on the roof to the left of the front door. It had fallen off a tree some time ago and was hanging down off the roof. While it was easily within reach, nobody removed it. The twig wasn't a danger to anyone, but it was certainly an eyesore. Every day for months, the manager walked past the tree limb. Was he simply not a detailed person? Was he deep in thought about his to-do list each day when he passed by the twig to walk through the front door? Did he need to partner with a detail-oriented teammate or create a simple process to scan his branch environment regularly? Or did he just not care? If he wasn't the type of person to pick up the gum wrapper—or, in this case, a twig—how could he build a team of employees who were? As a leader, a critical element is that we ourselves are engaged. According to a study conducted by Gallup, only 35 percent of managers are engaged.[6] So only slightly more than a third of us are picking up the gum wrappers. The question we have to ask ourselves every day is: **Am I one of the 65 percent who walk by the tree limb, or am I one of the 35 percent who show my team the way to excellence?** As a side note, no one on that manager's team ever removed the tree limb.

CHANGE THE CONVERSATION, CHANGE THE WAY YOU LEAD

What we talk about is what we're focused on, and it tells those around us what we value. If we believe our job is to fix people to improve performance, we might compare one employee to another in an effort to show the lower-performing person how to do the job, which can cause jealousy and division. Approaching that same conversation drawing out how the lower-performing employee naturally does things and coaching within those preferences to help her perform at a higher level will end with the employee feeling understood and more committed. Along those lines, think about a team member who loves to talk because he's good at it, it helps

---

6   "State of the American Manager: Analytics and Advice for Leaders." *Gallup,* 2014, 8.

him think through ideas, and it gives him energy. It can also lead him to unintentionally dominate conversations, making others feel unheard. If the culture we've created is rooted in appreciation for natural gifts, our team is more likely to give him grace in the future because they know he needs to work through thoughts verbally. At the same time, because he now knows this about himself he can pull back a bit when he feels himself taking over a meeting or a discussion. When the team talks about his incredible ability to articulate, no one is rolling their eyes or calling him a blabbermouth under their breath. The discussion is more positive, productive, and accepting.

Here are two interrelated metaphors to keep in mind when having conversations with your team:

People are like stars. We all have unique points of power (i.e., our strengths) and we all also have gaps in between our points of power (i.e., our weaknesses). As leaders, we can build a winning culture by focusing on helping team members grow their points of power, not directing them to work on the gaps where they lack talent. Instead, consider compensating for one person's weakness by leveraging the strengths of a colleague. In your mind's eye, see their stars interlocking with the point of one star inserted into the gap of the other. This approach paints a picture of success by building on our strengths to make our individual and collective stars shine more brightly.

If we have a sailboat and that boat has a leak we'd be crazy not to fix it, because the boat will sink otherwise. However, even if we fix the leak, we're not going to go anywhere until we unfurl the sails and let the wind take us. Think about the hole as a weakness and the sail as a strength. We need to figure out a way to manage our weaknesses but spend the bulk of our time investing in our strengths and the strengths of the people on our team, for that is where top shelf performance resides.

LEARN ABOUT EMPLOYEE UNIQUENESS WITH CLIFTONSTRENGTHS

CHAPTER 3

___

WE'RE ALL UNIQUE

Each person has gifts they bring to the team. As leaders, our goal is to understand, appreciate, and leverage those natural talents. That is how we get the best from people so they excel and become more fulfilled, collaboration becomes more fruitful, and organizations become stronger and more profitable. **Accordingly, our mindset as leaders when we look into the eyes of a team member must be: it's not how smart you are; it's how you're smart.**

That's why we start this process using the Clifton-Strengths Assessment, which we'll use at three different levels. First, it leads to greater self-awareness, a cornerstone of personal mastery and emotional intelligence. Second, it helps everyone effectively manage their relationships productively. Finally, it gives us insight into the work we do that we're good at *and* enjoy.

You'll want to take this online assessment first and study your results. Gallup, the publisher of the assessment, offers a variety of effective learning tools to help you better understand your results. Once you become familiar with the assessment, you can have other members of your team take it. Irrespective of the size of your team, you can start slow and gradually introduce aspects of the strengths' philosophy and people's results.

The availability of information provided by Gallup is what makes the instrument so useful. On Gallup's website, there is a personalized report, the Strengths Insight Guide, that is written specifically for you based on your responses to the assessment's 177 items. There is also the CliftonStrengths 34 Report, which offers a detailed explanation of your dominant talents and suggestions on how to handle the innate talents that are less intense for you. The site also has a number of videos that help you interpret your results. Additionally, Gallup sells numerous tools that will assist you in effectively using this newfound knowledge about your talents. You can also hire a Gallup Certified Strengths Coach, who can guide you through the process for a fee. A directory of coaches is provided on the same site as the assessment.

Understanding the nuances of each person requires observation, reflection, and discussion, so it's important to go deep and not gloss over this. **This is a process that**

requires depth not speed. When we get the subtle differences right, our relationships transform. If there's any question that people are all different, take a look at the numbers: when it comes to the CliftonStrengths Assessment, the odds of two people having the same top five Strengths but in a different order are 278,256 to 1. The odds of finding two people with the same top five Strengths in the same order—an exact blueprint of each other—are over 33,390,000 to 1, and that number grows exponentially when we consider the remainder of someone's dominant Strengths. Think about that for a second: we will never find two employees who are exactly alike. Those differences can be a distinct advantage when it comes to performance.

Rather than fighting against the uniqueness of our team members—i.e., trying to fill the gaps in their stars instead of focusing on their points of power—we're better served putting that talent to full use to achieve our goals. When we understand all people are simply wired differently, it can help us understand their behaviors in a way that allows us to give them the benefit of the doubt—a move that ultimately builds trust, decreases workplace conflict, and propels us toward producing better products and offering better services.

THE CLIFTONSTRENGTHS ASSESSMENT

There are many personality tests on the market, and

they all have their benefits. To me, the CliftonStrengths Assessment stands out from the crowd. Gallup, widely known for its polls and employee selection research, developed numerous semi-structured interviews to identify talent that could be enhanced and used to pursue positive outcomes in work and school. **The research began with a question asked by the inventor, Don Clifton, an educational psychologist at the University of Nebraska. What if we study what was *right* with people?** After four decades of research and over two million interviews, the CliftonStrengths Assessment was published in 1998. That, in part, is why I use it and recommend it. It's rooted in research and the study of excellence. It isn't based largely on theory or opinion.

The assessment measures innate talent in such a way that helps us predict how we'll act and react in situations, as well as helps us identify what we like and don't like to work on. It helps us figure out how our talent can be maximized to enhance performance and discover the road to living our best life. Like the sailboat analogy, it's not that we're saying to ignore our weaknesses but rather that we'll make significantly greater gains by focusing on our strengths.

To make that point, try this simple, quick experiment: sign your name on an open space in this book. Now, switch hands and sign your name again. How did that feel? Typically, when we write with our preferred hand, it's easy and natural. We don't even think about what we're doing. When we switch to our nondominant hand, it's typically clumsy, slower, and tends to be sloppy. Taking this a step further, if you were learning to sketch, it would be easier, quicker, and more comfortable to use your dominant hand than your nondominant hand. Greater improvement would also follow. That's the underlying philosophy behind strengths. When we invest energy in our strengths, the growth is exponential.

That same growth doesn't occur when we invest in our weaknesses. We'll improve, but marginally, and it will usually take us longer to gain that minimal uptick. Weaknesses are those things that drain us of energy and/or hamper our performance. Going back to the sailboat analogy and the hole in our boat, if a weakness is part of our job responsibilities, ignoring it would be foolish because it may sink us. We'd be better served partnering with someone who might have our weakness as a strength. Another solution might be to trade weaknesses with a colleague, where we take one of her tasks that our talents are more suited for and she takes our weakness that better fits her. **The point is not to avoid our weaknesses but to find productive solutions to overcome them.**

One of the things the assessment does better than any other is emphasize the differences in each of us in a positive way. As leaders, we can use this information to create a virtuous cycle of acceptance in the team where people are free to be themselves. When people are free to express their true nature, they are more likely to bring all of their personal power to their work without self-doubt or second-guessing. **CliftonStrengths changes the conversation from what people aren't doing right to what's right about them.**

For example, Peggy at my office has the talent theme of Consistency in the top five of her CliftonStrengths profile. I'll delve into what exactly each talent means later in this chapter, but one trait of people with Consistency high in their profile is they create and value sameness. That typically means treating people the same, which leads to a sense of fairness and being able to repeat processes the same way each time to ensure accuracy and efficiency. Consistency, for me, is a lesser talent and something I rarely think about. I'm unlikely to do the same thing the same way. Based on my talent themes, I'll tinker with what I've done in an effort to improve it for the next time. I'm also more inclined to treat everyone differently trying to make them feel special. This element of our personalities makes Peggy and me see some things very differently. Neither is better or worse; it's just who we are.

If I didn't understand the weight Peggy gives to fairness in the workplace, I could get irritated by some of her actions and priorities because they wouldn't match mine. Instead, because I know and understand this about her, I'm more open to consider how her perspective is beneficial. Conversely, because Peggy knows my tendencies, she is less likely to get annoyed when I make last-minute adjustments to something we're working on. She knows some of my best work happens during those eleventh-hour edits. Because we're aware of these things in each of us, we're then able to leverage our differences in ways that make both of us—and our company—better. For instance, if I'm about to make a decision that will impact a significant number of people in the company, I'll run it by Peggy to get her thoughts on whether she perceives it as fair to all of our colleagues. She'll give me her insight, which often makes me alter my approach. The tweaks may be minor but having Peggy's input makes the action I take more effective. That's the power of CliftonStrengths. Without the use of the assessment to understand the nuances of our personalities and the philosophy of playing to people's strengths, our working relationship would be far less collaborative. We've all experienced butting heads with someone in the office and realize how stressful and unproductive that is. But when we understand and appreciate each other's natural gifts and then intentionally leverage them, we both feel more valued, and our performance is better. **This is the foundation of a strengths-based workplace: people are free to be who they are and they're doing more of the work they're good at and enjoy.**

CLIFTONSTRENGTHS ASSESSMENT: THE LOGISTICS

The CliftonStrengths Assessment is an online instrument that can be accessed at gallupstrengthscenter.com. After you create an account and sign on, you'll need to purchase an access code, which at the time of this writing costs $19.99. This gives you access to your Top 5 Signature Themes. Once in, you'll respond to 177 items—each of which is timed at twenty seconds so you'll want to take the assessment at a time when you won't be interrupted. During their research, Gallup found that by timing the assessment at twenty seconds per item and by offering a choice between two positive pairs, people revealed their true self.

The assessment takes about forty-five minutes to complete. After your assessment is complete, you'll immediately have access to your results. The site offers a variety of reports and videos to help you better understand your talent themes.

Note: If you would like to see your entire profile of all 34 talent themes listed in order of intensity, you'll need to purchase an access code, which currently costs $49.99. This is money well spent, as this information can be transformative.

TALENTS, THEMES, AND STRENGTHS

I'm throwing a few different terms out—themes, talents, and strengths—that probably need clarification before we go any further. Even though the title is CliftonStrengths, the assessment actually measures talent themes. Talents are innate patterns of thoughts, feelings, and behaviors that must be used productively. As Don Clifton and his colleagues were doing their research and interviewing people in an effort to learn what made them successful, they found hundreds of talents were at play. Because the list was unmanageable, the researchers combined talents where similarities existed and culled the list to the most common thirty-four. (More about all thirty-four versus top five later.) Each of the thirty-four talent themes in the assessment is actually a rich nuance of talents. Think of themes like nesting dolls, each theme has a number of talents nestled inside it. As an example, some of the talents within the theme of Connectedness manifest themselves in these ways: providing acts of service, having the mindset that all things happen for a reason, knowing that we are all part of the same web of life so harm no one, be well-intentioned and create unity so there are no factions. Connectedness has a sense of calm about it, even during adversity, based on the conviction that everything happens for a reason. Connectedness is also gentle. The short definition of Connectedness is that people especially talented in the Connectedness theme have faith in the links among all things. They believe there are few coincidences and that almost every event has meaning.

While we do want to get talents into the everyday language of the team, we want to avoid using talent themes as labels. Labels can be a shorthand description that superficially and inaccurately describe a person. Typically, those labels are negative. A coworker might say, "Oh, that's just Conor's Connectedness," when he refuses to agree with a decision, which he foresees will cause a divide within the organization. While his talent of Connectedness certainly plays a role, Conor likely has several other reasons for his decision. Not the least of which is that he has a number of other dominant talent themes firing in this situation. We're all far too complicated to be labeled.

Talent themes become strengths when we use them productively. We turn our talents into strengths when we intentionally develop them to their fullest expression. A concrete way to think about this is using the formula: Talent x Investment = Strength. Investment can come in many forms: intentionality to avoid unproductive use, education, experimentation, deliberate practice, reflection, and seeking feedback.

Strength comes in two forms: *being* means who you are and *doing* means what you do. Turning your talents into strengths so you become the best version of yourself is "being," while "doing" is performing the work you're good at *and* enjoy. There's an important distinction to be made when it comes to doing: just because you're good at something doesn't make it a strength. We all learn to get good at tasks that we don't care about. We're smart, so we can figure out how to do many things well. We may need to do this for our own personal success or the success of our team or our company, but if we stopped doing these tasks tomorrow, we'd be just as happy.

As an example, Tuni loves to help her clients install the software that her company sells. She is a gifted communicator and has in-depth technical knowledge. Tuni's the go-to person in her company for this assignment. After working with the client, she has to invoice them for her time. While Tuni completes the invoices timely and accurately, she'd be very happy if someone else in her company would take this task from her. She's good at invoicing because she's figured out an efficient way to complete that particular task, but she doesn't enjoy doing it. Training clients on software installation is a strength; invoicing clients is not. That's an important distinction when we're thinking about strengths: **no joy equals no strength.**

A strength gives you energy and fulfillment when you perform it. You pick it up quickly, time flies by when you're in action, and you want to repeat it when you come back to work the next day.

It makes sense here to point out that it's difficult to spend every minute at work doing the things we're good at and enjoy. That said, one way to increase the use of strengths within the team is to realize that work one person finds dull might be satisfying to someone else. Judy is a department manager in a financial services business. As part of her job responsibilities, Judy is required to write policies—a task she dreads, although she is good at it.

Because she found the work to be awful, she didn't want to "dump" it on anyone else.

After going through the CliftonStrengths exercise with her team, Judy found Alex had the talent themes of Learner and Discipline. [People exceptionally talented in the Learner theme have a great desire to learn and want to improve continuously. The process of learning, rather than the outcome, excites them.] [People exceptionally talented in the Discipline theme enjoy routine and structure. Their world is best described by the order they create.]

In essence, he wanted to learn new things and was very precise. Alex had mentioned to Judy that he was looking for something new to learn, so I encouraged Judy to reach out to Alex and see if he might enjoy taking on some of her policy writing tasks. With his eye for detail and structure, writing policies had the potential to be in his sweet spot. That hunch turned out to be right. What Judy considered tedious and unfulfilling work, Alex was excellent at and found fun. He loved moving through the intricacies of policies. In the end, Alex was grateful Judy had enough confidence in him to delegate a task, and Judy was relieved to be rid of the duty knowing it would be done correctly and accurately.

CLIFTONSTRENGTHS TALENT THEMES

The following is a breakdown of each of the thirty-four talent themes. Remember, these parameters are rooted in decades of research from Gallup and form the basis of the CliftonStrengths Assessment. These definitions, as all of those previously noted, are cited from the Clifton-Strengths Themes Quick Reference Card.

- **Achiever®** : People exceptionally talented in the Achiever theme work hard and possess a great deal of stamina. They take immense satisfaction in being busy and productive.
- **Activator®**: People exceptionally talented in the Activator theme can make things happen by turning thoughts into action. They want to do things now, rather than simply talk about them.
- **Adaptability®**: People exceptionally talented in the Adaptability theme prefer to go with the flow. They tend to be "now" people who take things as they come and discover the future one day at a time.
- **Analytical®**: People exceptionally talented in the Analytical theme search for reasons and causes. They have the ability to think about all the factors that might affect a situation.
- **Arranger®**: People exceptionally talented in the Arranger theme can organize, but they also have a flexibility that complements this ability. They like to

determine how all of the pieces and resources can be arranged for maximum productivity.

+ **Belief®**: People exceptionally talented in the Belief theme have certain core values that are unchanging. Out of these values emerges a defined purpose for their lives.
+ **Command®**: People exceptionally talented in the Command theme have presence. They can take control of a situation and make decisions.
+ **Communication®**: People exceptionally talented in the Communication theme generally find it easy to put their thoughts into words. They are good conversationalists and presenters.
+ **Competition®**: People exceptionally talented in the Competition theme measure their progress against the performance of others. They strive to win first place and revel in contests.
+ **Connectedness®**: People exceptionally talented in the Connectedness theme have faith in the links among all things. They believe there are few coincidences and that almost everything has meaning.
+ **Consistency®**: People exceptionally talented in the Consistency theme are keenly aware of the need to treat people the same. They crave stable routines and clear rules and procedures that everyone can follow.
+ **Context®**: People exceptionally talented in the Context theme enjoy thinking about the past. They understand the present by researching its history.

- **Deliberative®**: People exceptionally talented in the Deliberative theme are best described by the serious care they take in making decisions or choices. They anticipate obstacles.

- **Developer®**: People exceptionally talented in the Developer theme recognize and cultivate the potential in others. They spot the signs of each small improvement and derive satisfaction from evidence of progress.

- **Discipline®**: People exceptionally talented in the Discipline theme enjoy routine and structure. Their world is best described by the order they create.

- **Empathy®**: People exceptionally talented in the Empathy theme can sense other people's feelings by imagining themselves in others' lives or situations.

- **Focus®**: People exceptionally talented in the Focus theme can take a direction, follow through, and make the corrections necessary to stay on track. They prioritize, then act.

- **Futuristic®**: People exceptionally talented in the Futuristic theme are inspired by the future and what could be. They energize others with their visions of the future.

- **Harmony®**: People exceptionally talented in the Harmony theme look for consensus. They don't enjoy conflict; rather, they seek areas of agreement.

- **Ideation®**: People exceptionally talented in the Ideation theme are fascinated by ideas. They are able to find connections between seemingly disparate phenomena.

+ **Includer®**: People exceptionally talented in the Includer theme accept others. They show awareness of those who feel left out and make an effort to include them.

+ **Individualization®**: People exceptionally talented in the Individualization theme are intrigued with the unique qualities of each person. They have a gift for figuring out how different people can work together productively.

+ **Input®**: People exceptionally talented in the Input theme have a need to collect and archive. They may accumulate information, ideas, artifacts, or even relationships.

+ **Intellection®**: People exceptionally talented in the Intellection theme are characterized by their intellectual activity. They are introspective and appreciate intellectual discussions.

+ **Learner®**: People exceptionally talented in the Learner theme have a great desire to learn and want to continuously improve. The process of learning, rather than the outcome, excites them.

+ **Maximizer®**: People exceptionally talented in the Maximizer theme focus on strengths as a way to stimulate personal and group excellence. They seek to transform something strong into something superb.

+ **Positivity®**: People exceptionally talented in the Positivity theme have contagious enthusiasm. They are upbeat and can get others excited about what they are going to do.

- **Relator®:** People exceptionally talented in the Relator theme enjoy close relationships with others. They find deep satisfaction in working hard with friends to achieve a goal.
- **Responsibility®:** People exceptionally talented in the Responsibility theme take psychological ownership of what they say they will do. They are committed to stable values such as honesty and loyalty.
- **Restorative®:** People exceptionally talented in the Restorative theme are adept at dealing with problems. They are good at figuring out what is wrong and resolving it.
- **Self-Assurance®.** People exceptionally talented in the Self-Assurance theme feel confident in their ability to manage their own lives. They have an inner compass that gives them certainty in their decisions.
- **Significance®:** People exceptionally talented in the Significance theme want to make a big impact. They are independent and prioritize projects based on how much influence they will have on their organization or people around them.
- **Strategic®:** People exceptionally talented in the Strategic theme create alternative ways to proceed. Faced with any given scenario, they can quickly spot the relevant patterns and issues.

- **WOO®**: People exceptionally talented in the WOO theme love the challenge of meeting new people and winning them over. They derive satisfaction from breaking the ice and making a connection with someone.

USING YOUR RESULTS STARTS WITH SELF-AWARENESS AND ENDS WITH INCREASED PERFORMANCE

After you've taken the assessment and studied your top five talent themes, it's time to use the results. The first key to leveraging this new information is greater self-awareness. One benefit of CliftonStrengths is that it shows us our inborn talents broken out individually. It's rare that we've ever thought about our abilities with such precision. We live our lives and do what we do. We respond to situations, most times, without deviation. **How we do some things can be how we do everything. We have to be careful because our reflexive response isn't always our best response.** By building our self-awareness, we can eliminate destructive habits or thought patterns that drag us down. As the African proverb reminds us, "When there is no enemy within, the enemies outside can do you no harm."

The assessment provides clarity on why we do what we do and how we do it. Two people in a similar situation might take the same action but have vastly different intrinsic motivators leading to that action. Two other people might have the same goal but will achieve it taking different paths. Once you've taken the assessment, the website provides you access to a variety of reports and videos that define your talents. Here are the reports:

* **Strengths Insight Report**, which is fully customized to you. This means that each paragraph of your top five talents is different than everyone else's. As an example, say you have the talent theme of Responsibility. [People exceptionally talented in the Responsibility theme take psychological ownership of what they say they will do. They are committed to stable values such as honesty and loyalty.] Even if your coworker shares that talent with you, your paragraphs in your Strengths Insight Reports will differ. That's because this report is written based on your responses to each of the 177 items.

* **The Signature Theme Report,** which provides you the generic full theme description of each of your Top 5 talents. In this report your paragraphs are not customized. So, if you have the talent of Achiever, the description will match everyone else's who has Achiever. [People exceptionally talented in the Achiever theme work hard and possess a great deal of stamina. They take immense satisfaction in being busy and productive.]

- **The Theme Sequence Report,** which provides you the list of all of your 34 talents in intensity order. Each talent is accompanied by the short definition. (The short definitions are the ones we have used in this book.) There is also a three-part video series that further explains the report.
- **The CliftonStrengths 34 Report** includes instructions for making the most of your dominant talent themes and navigating the rest. This report is the most comprehensive as it combines information from the previous three reports as well as listing potential blind spots to be aware of.

Gallup also has a library of YouTube videos featuring Gallup experts and seasoned Gallup certified coaches that further define and explain each of the thirty-four talents. There is so much information available. The only thing stopping you from discovering everything you can about your talents is YOU.

As you begin to recognize the capacity of your talent themes, you start to understand how they benefit you and how they can benefit the performance of your team and your organization. CliftonStrengths gives you the knowledge to play the cards you've been dealt to live your Royal Flush life. Here are a few examples:

When Jan took CliftonStrengths, things started to

make sense. One of her dominant talent themes was Communication. [People exceptionally talented in the Communication theme generally find it easy to put their thoughts into words. They are good conversationalists and presenters.] The edge that people with Communication have is that they are typically articulate, energized by discussions, and able to get their point across. This fit Jan to a T. She loved to have conversations with people and disliked silence. Her colleagues often complimented her ability to use the right words in any situation. As a result, an advantage she brought to the team was being their spokesperson on projects. Jan was able to fluently explain what the team had accomplished and how they went about it. But Jan had more to offer. As we discussed the power of Communication, Jan realized that while she had the additional skill to help others put their feelings and thoughts into words, she rarely did. We talked about how she could begin to help others find the words to best express themselves.

At their next team meeting, Jan volunteered to assist anyone who was having difficulty formulating their words in a given circumstance. Whether it was a delicate situation, a stressful interaction, or simply a conversation that required the right words to make the point clearly, Jan could help. Teammates began to take Jan up on her offer. Jan enjoyed working with her colleagues, and they benefitted from her coaching. Their interactions went more smoothly than ever before. With Jan's help, the team's influence in the company rose. Efficiency also soared as fewer meetings were needed because the content was on point and expectations were clear. Word got out in the company (pun intended) about Jan's prowess and people from other departments began to contact her for advice. Eventually, Jan became known in the company as the "Communication Consultant," as many looked to her for help when they needed to deliver the right message.

Ed's CliftonStrengths results showed he was high on the Ideation talent theme. [People exceptionally talented in the Ideation theme are fascinated by ideas. They are able to find connections between seemingly disparate phenomena.] The edge this gave Ed was his creativity and ability to see the possibility in things. This explained why Ed always loved brainstorming sessions. Ed said his wife often told him he had as many ideas as there were blades of grass on their lawn. Many would seek Ed's advice when they were stuck in their work and needed a fresh perspective. As we talked about the Ideation talent theme, Ed mentioned he was drawn to the newest technology, so we discussed ways he might lend this ability to his colleagues. Even though Ed didn't work in the IT department, he offered to act as the office guinea pig for any new devices or operating systems the company planned to roll out. This paid dividends, too, as Ed was able to provide novel suggestions from an end user's perspective. The

IT team began to rely on Ed for his suggestions and they produced better products because of it.

Betty's CliftonStrengths results showed WOO as one of her dominant talents. [People exceptionally talented in the WOO theme love the challenge of meeting new people and winning them over. They derive satisfaction from breaking the ice and making a connection with someone.] Betty derived great satisfaction from breaking the ice and making a connection with someone. When her work took her to a networking event, she thrived. She easily floated around the room talking with people. She left a trail of smiles and goodwill behind as she moved from one person to the next. Because of this ability, Betty developed a vast professional network on whom she called when she needed expertise. This network not only benefited Betty, but her company reaped the benefit of many new customers and referral sources. As we talked about her WOO, I explained that one of the traits of this talent theme is that you can develop a substantial amount of influence by coupling people in your network who need assistance. This opened Betty's eyes to something she never considered: proactively linking those in her network to one another as well as her colleagues. Betty consistently used her network for her own needs but only occasionally put people together when one could help another. Betty realized that she used her WOO reactively but could be of greater support to others if she was more proactive in her matchmaking. Using her new approach, Betty eventually increased her network, enhanced her reputation, and gained greater influence.

These examples begin to illustrate the three-dimensional benefit of using CliftonStrengths. As mentioned, the first is greater self-awareness. Most times we respond in ways that are automatic. We think of something and we act in a way that makes sense to us or we may not see an opportunity in front of us because it's out of our normal pattern of responses.

When we have names to describe our actions and reactions, we have something concrete that can guide us to make better decisions. Jan's decision to coach people became a critical moment in her development. This impacts the second level: how we work with those around us. When we're more aware of ourselves, we can be better teammates. We start to see how we can modify our approach to make the situation better. If we really understand our teammates, we can also leverage them, like the IT department did with Ed in that last example. The third level is the actual work we do. These are our "doing" strengths, like the example of Betty increasing her influence in her network, which increased the revenue she generated.

USING THE ASSESSMENT RESULTS AS A TEAM

Hopefully, you can see how the assessment is useful for you as an individual leader, and you will gain even greater momentum when you share this amazing tool with your team. That's when the real magic happens. I've used the assessment with small teams to organizations with over 12,000 employees. Irrespective of the size of your team or organization, the simple way to begin is by having your immediate team take the assessment. You can gradually expand from there.

Your team members should follow the same learning path that you did—take the assessment and study the online tools covering their results. Once members become familiar with their results, a good first step is to have each person highlight the words, phrases, and sentences that resonate in their Strengths Insight Report (the personalized report) and share it with the rest of the team. Prioritizing time to have people meet in pairs to discuss what they've read about each other begins a meaningful dialogue that's anchored in success and positive attributes. You'll want to participate in these meetings and set the expectation that everyone should be prepared and open-minded. It's critical that you model the behaviors you expect. The process for the meetings looks like this:

♦ Prior to the meeting, both colleagues will want to read the other person's report.

- During the meeting, take turns sharing what you read in the report that matches what you see in your colleague, especially the sections that aren't highlighted. Sometimes, others see things in us that we don't see in ourselves.
- Also take turns asking questions to gain a better understanding of your colleague's talent themes and how you can best work together. Some questions to start that discussion might include:
  - How do you see yourself using your talent themes at the office?
  - How can I help you have your best day at work?
  - What do I do that might cause you stress? How can I mitigate that?

These meetings can have a profound impact on relationships because people are having purposeful conversations they rarely have. Even if your team has worked together for several years, you will learn things about each other that you didn't know. You'll also begin to understand why people do the things they do and why they do them the way they do. The following example is a common occurrence I've witnessed in my experience working with hundreds of teams and more than 10,000 employees: two people worked together for over seven years in a small company. Sean worked in operations, and Sarah worked in sales. While they were on different teams, they worked closely together. Before we rolled out Clifton-

Strengths, they tolerated one another—on a good day. Typically, when Sarah used her Strategic talent theme, Sean's Analytical talent theme would immediately begin to question her approaches. [People exceptionally talented in the Strategic theme create alternative ways to proceed. Faced with any given scenario, they can quickly spot the relevant patterns and issues.] [People exceptionally talented in the Analytical theme search for reasons and causes. They have the ability to think about all of the factors that might affect a situation.] When this happened, Sarah became defensive, feeling that Sean didn't think her solutions would work. Sean became irritated with Sarah because she couldn't thoroughly answer all of his questions, and she refused to gather data to support her assertion. Their relationship didn't dramatically transform immediately after they took the assessment, but as each of them began to gain a greater understanding of the other, small improvements in their working relationship took place. In meetings when Sarah threw out a solution, Sean didn't immediately begin to question her. He sat back and listened. When Sean looked for facts from Sarah to support her thinking, she researched instead of pushing back.

The watershed moment, though, occurred about four months into our work on talent themes when Sean sent Sarah an email in response to a client's question. Sarah interpreted Sean's email as curt, negative, and confrontational. "Same old Sean," she initially thought. Before they took CliftonStrengths, Sarah would have forwarded the email to her boss, who would have then forwarded it to Sean's boss. Sean's boss would have sat down with him and discussed the tone of his email. Of course, this would have led to Sean being angry at Sarah, and their relationship would have deteriorated further. Instead of following the entrenched pattern of behavior, Sarah realized that Sean's intent was to be factual and direct so Sarah would understand the issue. Looking at the email through Sean's eyes gave Sarah a whole new perspective. Instead of firing off an email to her manager, she walked over to Sean's office to discuss it. They resolved the issue quickly and amicably. Sarah noticed that while they were discussing the problem, Sean was supportive, not combative. Their relationship continues to grow to this day. As in all strengths-based environments, teamwork blossomed and, with it, efficiency. **When we approach a colleague like a wrecking ball, we leave rubble, but when we appreciate our colleague, we build a unified house.**

There are many more reasons a strengths-based environment is a better environment, as cited in Gallup's State of the American Manager:

+ Employees who learn to use their strengths are 7.8 percent more productive.

- For employees who agree that their manager focuses on their strengths, the odds of them throwing the gum wrapper on the floor decreases to 1 percent.
- Teams that receive strengths feedback have 8.9 percent greater profitability.
- Teams that focus on strengths everyday increase their productivity by 12.5 percent.

The statistics are eye opening. The results we can achieve are even more compelling. Additionally, the intangible outcomes—like camaraderie, true collaboration, and unity—are potent factors that build a culture where people are picking up the gum wrapper.

ACTIONABLE TOOLS FOR YOU, YOUR TEAM, AND YOUR ORGANIZATION

Once your team members complete the Clifton-Strengths Assessment, it's time to put the results into action. The stories I shared above would never have been possible if every member of the team didn't study their own strengths and understand the results of their colleagues.

There are a number of ways you can begin to use the results of the assessment within your team. As noted above, a good first step is having every member of the team share their Strengths Insight Reports and have a discussion about the information. That activity is detailed in the Appendix.

Another action which you can take even before the reviews of each person's Strengths Insight Report is to have everyone come prepared to a team meeting to discuss their answers to questions like these:

- What was your initial reaction to your results?
- Did anything surprise you?
- What resonated with you?
- How can we use this information to increase our effectiveness?

To make this meeting valuable, you will want to have people come prepared by studying their reports and watching the videos. It can also prove helpful to provide the discussion questions in advance of the meeting so people have time to think through their answers.

Please don't make the mistake of cramming everything in to one meeting and assuming you're finished. We've all experienced those situations in our careers. An assessment is introduced, we read it, talk about it for an hour at a meeting and then put it in a folder never to be seen again. CliftonStrengths is a tool that will transform interactions and productivity, so you want to squeeze out every last drop of learning. Take as much care and effort with this process as you would your most important project. If you only get to a couple of people's results in this first meeting, that's fine; pick it up at the next meeting. It's most effective to devote small amounts of time over dozens of meetings. **This isn't something to "check off the box." Slow and deep is better than fast and finished.** We as leaders should go first in discussing our results so we can model the effort, energy, and enthusiasm we want every member of the team to approach this with. Our level of preparation and thought should be evident.

In subsequent meetings, everyone can share and discuss their Signature Theme Report, which provides the generic full theme descriptions of each person's Top 5. Once everyone gains a clear understanding of their Top 5 talent themes and how to apply them for their greatest success, everyone can work through the remainder of their dominant talents. Dominant talent themes are those which guide our thoughts, feelings, and behaviors on a daily basis. The number of these can vary by person. While the Top 10 is the statistically valid number based on Gallup's research, in my experience, many people can claim up to the Top 13 as dominant. The CliftonStrengths 34 Report becomes our main tour guide once we go past our Top 5. It's also beneficial for everyone to study the full theme descriptions for the remainder of their dominant talents and watch any of the Gallup videos available on YouTube. People can begin to develop action plans on how they can use their dominant talents to perform at a high level and live their most fulfilling life. When you reach the Leadership Practices section of the book, you'll find additional tools, which will help everyone on the team optimize the use of their Strengths.

Once you've exhausted reviewing everyone's reports, here are a few other tools that can prove helpful. You can be the best judge of when to introduce these to the team.

THE NEEDS ACTIVITY

You likely have read the work done by Abraham Maslow on his hierarchy of needs. While his theory was first published in 1943, his hierarchy of needs is timeless and is still covered today in education and training courses. Along those lines, our talent themes have a unique set of needs. Having our needs met is vital to our happiness. We want to come alongside and help where we can. The more our needs get met at work, the better we feel, and the more productive we usually are. Meeting another's needs cements the relationship because it's a way to show a person you accept her for who she is and value what's important to her. **We never want to resent someone for trying to get their needs met.**

The Needs Activity provides a vehicle to raise the idea of talent needs and how we might be able to meet them.

In this activity, each talent theme has a one-line need associated with it. For example, the Achiever need is "freedom to get work done on my own schedule," and the Futuristic need is "opportunities to talk and think about the future." (For a full list, please visit the Appendix.)

Prior to a team meeting, give each person a copy of the Needs Activity worksheet and ask each one to check off their top five talent themes. Next, have each person rate how frequently she feels her needs get met at work using the provided scale of one to five, with five being high. At the meeting, have people work in pairs to discuss their ratings and answer the two questions at the bottom of the activity worksheet. Next, have each member of the team provide their answers to the entire team. The real key to this activity is to see what can be done to ensure all members of the team have their needs met more frequently. More than any other, this activity, when followed by action, shows all members of your team the value you place on them because you're doing something that's important to their well-being. It's more about making work comfortable and appealing. An indirect benefit is that performance typically gets a lift as well.

Here are three examples of outcomes from this activity, which you can also use when explaining it to your team. The shifts in these examples not only made life easier for the person, but the team benefitted from a more confident colleague.

A person had the Deliberative talent theme in his Top 5. [People exceptionally talented in the Deliberative theme are best described by the serious care they take in making decisions or choices. They anticipate obstacles.] This person said he felt he was rushed into some decisions; therefore, he rated the need for Deliberative—time to weigh the pros and cons before needing to decide—a two on a scale of one to five. This led to an insightful discussion about how his team could give him a little more time to decide by getting information to him earlier in the process. The end result was that his decisions were better and he felt more at ease when deciding.

In another team, a member had the Analytical talent theme in her Top 5 and rated as a one. [People exceptionally talented in the Analytical theme search for answers and causes. They have the ability to think about all of the factors that might affect a situation.] She asked her team to flood her with information. An insightful colleague pointed out that her need for data was why she asked so many questions when people came to her. The team adjusted, and the person with Analytical was appreciative. Not only that, but her comfort and overall performance increased because she felt like she was getting what she needed to make effective decisions.

One person had the Adaptability talent theme in his Top 5. [People exceptionally talented in the Adaptability theme prefer to go with the flow. They tend to be "now" people who take things as they come and discover the future one day at a time.] He rated the need—present pressure that demands an immediate response—a three. For him, the need was about waiting until the due date to complete a given assignment. Although he never missed a deadline, many of his colleagues would constantly check on his progress when they were working on a joint project. The check-ins became a source of frustration for him. It wasn't that he was procrastinating; the pressure of the deadline increased his intensity and will to finish what was needed. Once this became clear to his coworkers, they accepted his work style and were relieved to no longer follow up with him. What was once a mild bone of contention among the team dissolved.

One other note on this activity: as leaders we should share our needs last. Symbolically, it says something when we're discussing what people need and we, as leaders, put others' needs before our own.

THE EDGE ACTIVITY

The Edge Activity is all about leveraging the contributions from each talent theme. Edge is all about the power you bring. The Edge Activity lists contributions from each talent theme. For example, the Empathy talent theme's Edge includes these traits: "creates trust, brings healing, knows just what to say/do in a given situation, and customizes the approach to others' emotional needs," while the Strategic talent theme's Edge include these traits: "anticipates alternatives, intuitive, sees different paths." (A full list is found in the Appendix.)

Similar to the Needs Activity, prior to a team meeting, provide everyone a copy of the Edge Activity worksheet (found in the Appendix). Ask your team members to note their top five talent themes and then underline any or all of the contributions that resonate with them. At the meeting, have people take turns sharing with the whole team what they've underlined. After a person reads her list of contributions, colleagues should comment where they've seen this person demonstrate some or all of those characteristics.

It is also interesting to have colleagues review the words a person *didn't* underline to see if there are contributions the person didn't give herself credit for. This happens frequently, and it's very uplifting when colleagues point out positive attributes they see in one another. After you've taken the necessary time to complete this activity with the utmost attention, ask each person to come up with actions they can take to leverage these contributions. If these are some of the best attributes that team members have to offer, we want to get the most out of each person. Remember this is the powerful Edge that people have to offer the team. In my experience, it is around these contributions where you want to ratchet up expectations.

Stretch goals tied to what someone already does well are exhilarating. For example, Melanie had the Activator talent theme in her Top 5 and saw herself as an "energy source" who was good at taking action. [People exceptionally talented in the Activator theme can make things happen by turning thoughts into action. They want to do things now, rather than simply talk about them.] Her colleagues all agreed. Melanie's manager talked with her in the team meeting while doing this activity and asked if she would be the person on the team who jumped in when she felt like the team was getting bogged down on an issue. Melanie loved the idea and flourished in the role. Over time, she perfected the exact right time to move the team from discussion to action. Everyone on the team appreciated her moving things along, and the team became more productive as a result. This is a confidence-boosting individual activity, but there is substantial merit to the collective group as well because it allows colleagues to see where each person can excel.

THE OVERUSE ACTIVITY

Up until now, we've been discussing the power of our

talent themes. The reality is our talent themes are neutral, and it's up to us to use them productively. This is why the formula we referenced earlier, Strength = Talent x Investment, is so important. We've got to take the potential our talent themes gives us and work to make the themes as powerful as they can be. It's also why understanding the nuances of our talent themes is critical to avoid getting derailed at times. If we look at the talent theme of Command, the Edge includes these traits: charismatic, direct, driven, inspirational, easy to follow, clear, concise, to the point. [People exceptionally talented in the Command theme have presence. They can take control of a situation and make decisions.] Now for that same talent theme of Command, let's look at the shadow side attributes: bossy, domineering, rude, abrupt, short, strong-willed, inflexible, stubborn. (Find a full list in the Overuse Activity, located in the Appendix.) These are two sides of the same coin. If Command is a dominant talent and we lack self-awareness, we will dull the Edge Command can bring and leave an unpleasant wake behind us. **Leaving a wake of some sort is true for every talent. Any talent theme overused can become a liability.**

Working with the CliftonStrengths Assessment since 2004, I've often found that what trips people up is what's at the top of their Strengths Profile, not what's at the bottom. For example, Anna Mae has the talent theme of Learner in her Top 5, so she has a great desire to continuously learn and improve and is inspired by the process of learning. [People exceptionally talented in the Learner theme have a great desire to learn and want to continuously improve. The process of learning, rather than the outcome, excites them.] This serves her well because it drives her to a level of expertise in her field that is envied by her colleagues. However, when she overuses this talent theme and sees herself as the expert among her peers, Anna Mae won't listen to their thoughts and ideas because she feels they don't know as much as she does. She can come across as a know-it-all. Since receiving feedback, Anna Mae has worked hard not to dismiss others and to be more open to their opinions and suggestions.

To complete the Overuse Activity, distribute the document prior to a team meeting and have each team member review the characteristics associated with each of their Top 5 and underline those they believe to be true about them. At the team meeting, have each person discuss the one characteristic from their list, which, if corrected, would have the greatest impact on performance and/or relationships. The questions on the worksheet can be used to generate discussion. In this activity, we as leaders should go first. Depending on the degree of safety within the team, this can be an uncomfortable activity for people, and we can show every member of the team that it's ok not to be perfect.

No one is and as a team we must be vulnerable with one another and support one another.

At the heart of this activity are two objectives: the first is heightened self-awareness to stop unproductive behavior; the second, creating an environment where team members are at ease offering feedback to their colleagues to help them eliminate unproductive behavior when they slip. **That's the essence of a team—people pick each other up when they err and come alongside to help them make the correction that benefits the person and advances the team.** This all takes time, but gradually people begin to recognize their own overuse and adjust. Then people start to offer each other supportive feedback. This is made easier when people make a point to request feedback during the activity. As leaders, a milestone moment can occur when we make the first request. For many teams, giving feedback eventually becomes natural in other aspects of their work and overall performance increases.

Here's what this looks like in practice for Anna Mae if she might be overusing her Learner talent theme in a meeting by constantly interrupting Julian without letting him finish his thoughts. Following the meeting, we could approach Anna Mae and say, "I might be misreading the situation, but it seemed like you overused your Learner just now. It felt to me like you kept cutting off Julian when he was commenting on your area of expertise. Did you feel that way?" If more questions are appropriate, we could ask:

* When he was talking did you feel challenged by his comments?
* Did you feel like you had to assert your expertise?
* Did you think he was wrong in his thinking?
* Would you do anything differently the next time?

How you handle the situation depends heavily on how you're wired and your relationship, but questions are a non-accusatory way to help someone recognize unproductive behavior. In these cases, we aren't trying to change our colleague, but rather help her regulate ineffective behavior.

Team members should also provide positive reinforcement when they see a colleague intentionally act to stop overuse. This can get overlooked when we're on watch for overuse. Since it's tough to change our behavior, creating an environment which nurtures the effort people are making to be better and do better is crucial to everyone's success.

TALENT THEMES GIVE US STRENGTHS

We've spent a lot of this chapter discussing talent themes

as they relate to self-awareness and interactions, and we don't want to forget that talent themes draw us to work at which we excel. Those are our strengths—what we enjoy and we're good at. The tools we've been discussing can indirectly generate conversation about the work we do, and there are tools in the upcoming leadership section that will be useful to hone in on people's strengths. Playing to strengths is the number one action we as leaders can take to increase everyone's commitment to pick up the gum wrapper. **Think about this for a second: people don't burn out from working too hard, they burn out from working too hard at things they don't enjoy.** When we're really enjoying something we're doing, we aren't usually complaining about it and drained; we're energized and upbeat.

We can't let roles and job descriptions determine how to put people's strengths to work. Those can be too limiting and inhibit performance. Not everyone in the same role is going to enjoy or excel at the same types of activities, just the way you and your friends didn't all lunge for the same Halloween candy when you were young. Think back to your childhood for a moment: for me, as a kid, I'd go trick-or-treating and take my bag of loot to a friend's house along with several others in my group. We'd dump our bags of candy on the floor where one friend would grab his Reese's cups, another would go for the Milky Ways, and I'd snatch the Baby Ruths. We'd go around the room so all of us got the candy we liked best. We'd always have things none of us wanted, like an apple or a toothbrush (from the neighborhood dentist) but we'd divvy it up and stuff it into our bags just the same.

This metaphor can actually be put into practice in the office when it comes to the work everyone does. Here is a fantastic example of a manager being open to every member of the team playing to their strengths and blurring the lines between roles and job descriptions to create a high performing team who loves to come to work each morning.

Steve managed a bank branch inside chain grocery stores—a once common scene in the banking industry, partly because the repeat customer base is built-in. The average person goes to the grocery store two and a half times a week, and they're more likely to form relationships with familiar faces they see at the branch during each visit to buy groceries, as the branch is usually positioned by the store's entrance. A strategy employed at grocery store branches is to have the bank employees walk through the aisles talking with people as they shop for groceries. The thinking goes that as the employees become familiar with shoppers they can eventually sell them on the idea of banking at the branch because it's convenient. However, most bankers don't like walking down the cereal aisle, see a customer buying Cheerios, and say, "I like Cheerios, too. Would you like to open a checking account?" That kind of interaction goes beyond awkward.

Steve was one of four employees in the branch, which was struggling. The team was way behind on all their performance goals, and morale was low, as most didn't want to walk the aisles but were forced to do it as part of the branch's growth strategy. Because the majority of employees were uncomfortable, they would walk up and down the aisles reading product labels or positioning themselves in one place and feign smiles to shoppers passing by. Other times, they'd bag groceries, which helped the store but didn't do much to generate sales. Steve asked if I could take the team through the CliftonStrengths Assessment to find a way to improve performance and boost morale. As we discussed everyone's Top 5, we found something interesting that had not previously come to light.

Steve's talent themes of Analytical and Developer made him an ideal candidate to work with customers who wanted to borrow money. [People exceptionally talented in the Analytical theme search for reasons and causes. They have the ability to think about the factors that might affect a situation.] [People exceptionally talented in the Developer theme recognize and cultivate the potential in others. They spot the signs of each small improvement and derive satisfaction from evidence of progress.] Steve was proficient in math and relished studying data to find an answer, both traits of the Analytical talent theme. With Developer, he enjoyed helping customers improve their financial well-being and their lives by consolidating debt. This talent also made him an ideal coach and the main reason he was promoted to manager.

Carson's talents of Relator and Context in his Top 5 drove him to learn about people and understand their past and how they got where they are today. [People exceptionally talented in the Relator theme enjoy close relationships with others. They find deep satisfaction in working hard with friends to achieve a goal.] [People exceptionally talented in the Context theme enjoy thinking about the past. They understand the present by researching its history.] Carson liked nothing more than sitting with people and learning about them. This allowed him to build deep and lasting relationships with people. His sincerity and genuine curiosity built trust with customers.

Based on Brooke's talents of WOO and Connectedness in her Top 5, she enjoyed striking up conversations with people and being of service to others. [People exceptionally talented in the WOO theme love the challenge of meeting new people and winning them over. They derive satisfaction from breaking the ice and making connections with someone.] [People exceptionally talented in the Connectedness theme have faith in the links among all things. They believe there are few coincidences and that almost every event has meaning.] To her, walking the aisles had been fun. She easily interacted with shoppers and found ways to always leave them with a favorable impression of her and the bank. She had a gentle way that was disarming.

In Emily's Top 5 were Achiever and Discipline. [People exceptionally talented in the Achiever theme work hard and possess a great deal of stamina. They take immense satisfaction in being busy and productive.] [People exceptionally talented in the Discipline theme enjoy routines and structure. Their world is best described by the order they create.] Emily liked checking everything off her list with minimal interruptions. While aisle duty had been a nightmare for her, she excelled when she had the opportunity to crank through all the daily routines needed to run a branch.

As we discussed everyone's talents and how they manifested themselves into strengths, a specialized pattern of work distribution emerged. Brooke would spend four days each week walking the aisles. Any new customers would be given to Carson, who would learn about the person, build the relationship and open the account. Emily would work behind the scenes and handle all of the paperwork and daily operational and compliance tasks.

Steve would handle all loans and be the team's coach. Like any job, there were times people had to complete tasks that fell outside of these responsibilities. And there were tasks that no one wanted to do, so the team made a collective decision to rotate those so everyone shared the burden. But those times didn't weigh anyone down because they had set a team goal that each of them would spend 75 percent of their time playing to their strengths. And they stuck to it.

Prior to using this strengths-based approach, each employee spent one day a week walking the aisles. Except for Brooke, this was lost time for the rest of the team. Productivity suffered because three-quarters of the team were ill-suited for a major function of their jobs. When we shifted work to match the natural talents of the team members, productivity rose by 30 percent in the first full quarter following the change! Morale skyrocketed, too. This is the power we as leaders have. We can create strengths-based work that allows our colleagues to soar with their strengths!

TRUST THE PROCESS

Oscar Wilde said, "Be yourself. Everyone else is taken," a quote that speaks to the whole idea of strengths. When you create a dynamic within your team that embraces what makes each person special, it builds confidence. Confidence is a powerful force when it comes to high achievement.

Taking the CliftonStrengths Assessment and using it as a tool to help your people is only one part of the process of creating a team of people who pick up the gum wrapper.

While CliftonStrengths shows how we're all different, it's equally important to understand how we can all be the same.

In the next chapter, we'll explore the benefit of creating Behavioral Expectations, which serve as anchor points for interactions.

IDENTIFY COMPANY BEHAVIORAL EXPECTATIONS

CHAPTER 4

WHAT SIMILARITIES DRIVE YOUR ORGANIZATION?

You've got unique individuals in your company, but it's not until that group of individuals becomes a team that you optimize your results. If it was only about individual talent, a team sport like basketball would be played one-on-one. Focusing on similarities can be just as important as leveraging unique strengths when it comes to creating a healthy workplace, and one way to accomplish this goal is to create Behavioral Expectations (BEs). **Behavioral Expectations are a set of agreed upon codes of conduct that bring together a group of unique individuals and create predictability in how they interact with one another. In short, Behavioral Expectations serve as a North Star for unity, allowing team members to**

be who they are while honoring how they work with one another. Whereas the CliftonStrengths Assessment says, "Here's how we're unique," Behavioral Expectations say, "Here's how we're all the same." Both are equally important to understand and leverage.

Many companies call Behavioral Expectations core values, but that terminology doesn't describe exactly what we're trying to accomplish. The difference is core values don't always address how employees will interact with one another. Core values can often be vague or include attributes or attitudes that are customer-facing and promotional. Examples of core values I've seen are: Customer Service, Product Efficiency, and Continuous Process Improvement. While you can argue that these indirectly define how employees work together, I'm after something more concrete that provides direct guidance in how everyone should interact. If your team or company has solidly established core values that steer everyone's behavior in a straightforward manner, those should serve our purpose here. I'm not trying to make more work; if you've got something in place that's effective, keep it. In most companies, though, the core values are not known by most employees and lived by far fewer. I prefer the term Behavioral Expectations because it is truer to the process. Arriving at Behavioral Expectations is a monumental achievement for a team or an organization because they've created and committed to live by rules that govern how they'll treat one another. In a company with firmly established Behavioral Expectations, employees with entirely different work styles and methods of communicating can still feel confident they'll be treated consistently and fairly in every interaction. Problems occur when there aren't any expectations around people's behavior. As an example, in one company I worked for, there were no Behavioral Expectations. That meant pretty much any behavior was acceptable. The CEO was very focused on bottom-line results. He didn't seem to think much about how those results were achieved—just that they were achieved. This led to a divided leadership team as each leader was concerned only with the results for which they were responsible. As one leader told me, "The CEO only talks to me about my results so that's all I care about. My peers can worry about their results." Of course, this thinking permeated the leadership team and created a siloed organization. In one particularly nasty meeting, which was indicative of how people treated one another, the Chief Revenue Officer eviscerated the Chief Marketing Officer, telling half-truths about how his team had handled the marketing of a system conversion. The Chief Revenue Officer seemed to take great pleasure in making the Chief Marketing Officer squirm as he defended himself against one onslaught after another. The Chief Marketing Officer, tired of playing defense, fought back. For the next fifteen minutes, grenades were lobbed from both sides. As was par for this organization, nothing productive occurred from the meeting.

The twenty employees in attendance, representing various functions and levels, left the meeting battered and bruised. The work environment was a hornet's nest where the reality became attack or be attacked. Eventually, talented people began leaving the company finding more collaborative and harmonious organizations to join. Dysfunctional, the company sold a few years later, and that sale cost hundreds of remaining people their good-paying jobs.

To paint a contrasting picture, another company I worked for had a clear set of Behavioral Expectations. These were well-defined and frequently revisited by leaders throughout the organization and were labeled as "The Rules of Engagement." Two of these Behavioral Expectations were as follows:

- Give people the benefit of the doubt. Any of us can have a bad moment.
- Approach every situation in a positive, helpful way. You get what you give.

Driven by these guidelines, meetings never devolved into battles—and that's not to say that people didn't disagree. Rather, there were plenty of times when people debated viewpoints with rigor and passion. However, no one attacked, no one subverted, and everyone affirmed their colleagues by trying to understand the other's perspective. Meetings ended with clear decisions that everyone supported, even if they didn't totally agree. As you can imagine, the work environment felt like driving on a newly paved road, smooth and easy while heading toward your destination.

For Behavioral Expectations to be effective, they must be modeled by the leader and lived by everyone on the team. Additionally, what keeps Behavioral Expectations powerful is accountability. If everyone promises to interact in alignment with the Behavioral Expectations, then it's crucial to hold true to that commitment. I'm sure you've seen, and maybe worked in, organizations that have core values like honesty and courtesy emblazoned on their websites and printed on motivational posters in their offices. Yet if you observe employees in action, those core values don't match reality. I've experienced that, too. **That's why if we *properly* implement Behavioral Expectations, our day-to-day reality will match them.**

HOW BEHAVIORAL EXPECTATIONS WORK

Celebrating uniqueness in a strengths-based organization doesn't mean that we're giving anyone a pass when they behave poorly or in contradiction to the Behavioral Expectations.

For example, I worked with an organization that had a Behavioral Expectation of "Blamers are Drainers." This meant that casting blame was not useful to the team; what *was* useful was figuring out what went wrong and offering a solution. It also meant privately discussing an error with the person who made it to use it as a learning opportunity. Rick, a newly hired project manager, had the Restorative talent theme dominant in his CliftonStrengths Assessment results. People who are exceptionally talented in the Restorative theme are adept at dealing with problems. They are good at figuring out what is wrong and resolving it. In part, Rick's excellence came because he could see what wasn't working in every project he was assigned.

In Rick's previous company, people were rewarded for pointing out other's mistakes. This "gotcha" mentality ended up pitting employees against one another as each looked for another's error. Over time, the culture made Rick feel uncomfortable, so he left. Old habits die hard, though, and Rick continued pointing out what he viewed as others' mistakes in the new company without offering a solution or privately discussing the error with the person who made it. Because the new organization had so deeply embedded this Behavioral Expectation, colleagues were able to help Rick gradually recognize the accepted approach for dealing with problems. At first, Rick resisted, essentially saying, "This is how I am." To his credit, though, Rick adapted his behavior with the frequent coaching of his leader and his colleagues. Instead of coming to meetings pointing blame as he was accustomed, Rick began to prepare solutions to the issues he naturally spotted. He also met with others on the team who made an error to offer suggestions for preventing them in the future. **That's how Behavioral Expectations should work: people adapting their natural style to match the essence of the Behavioral Expectations so everyone brings their best to the team in a way that mirrors one another.**

As we learned when we discussed the CliftonStrengths Assessment, everyone is different. That means Rick and his colleagues will not interpret and apply Behavioral Expectations in exactly the same way. For example, Martha, another member of the team, may hear "Blamers are Drainers" and, based on her talent themes, feel as though she should never bring up anything that feels remotely negative because it might sound like she is blaming someone. This isn't in the spirit of the Behavioral Expectation, nor is it an effective way for Martha to best use her talent themes. Clearly defining what the Behavioral Expectation looks like in practice and repeatedly reviewing the root meaning based on actual situations is the way to bring as much alignment as possible within the team. **This continued clarifying and repeated "in the moment" coaching is usually the part organizations miss.** The merit of this approach is that Martha becomes likely to surface a problem and resolve it rather than hold back because she feels she will be viewed as a complainer. She lives the Behavioral Expectation because she understands what it looks like in action. Coaching takes courage. It's easier to make an excuse for a colleague or look the other way than to have a potentially difficult conversation; that's when the cracks in the foundation begin and those cracks are more likely to turn into chasms than repair themselves. **People aren't robots, but team members can behave in a way that is true to themselves while aligned with the real intention of the Behavioral Expectations.**

In this case, Rick may spot more problems by nature of his talent themes, while Martha may only point out more obvious problems. Each employee, in their own way, is properly applying the Behavioral Expectation.

CRAFTING SOLID BEHAVIORAL EXPECTATIONS

Behavioral Expectations should be easily remembered statements for how you expect those in your organization to act and communicate. They should not contain empty buzzwords. For example, many companies say, "Be respectful," or "Have integrity." Frankly, those are givens. If you don't have integrity, you shouldn't be able to work at a company, and you shouldn't be part of a team if you can't be respectful to others. The beauty of using catchy phrases, is that people remember them. For example, saying, "Blamers are Drainers," is more memorable than saying, "Don't blame other people for mistakes. Instead find a solution and present it and then make sure you follow up with the person who made the error and discuss ways to avoid that mistake in the future." While they mean the same thing, there is no comparison when it comes to which one gets remembered—and being remembered is the first step to living the Behavioral Expectation.

Creating catchy, meaningful, and succinct Behavioral Expectations is critical to the success of our unifying initiative because they form the anchor points for behavior within our organization. Behavioral Expectations provide stability in relationships and predictability in interactions—both of which lead to a foundational aspect of team success: trust. Stability and predictability are underrated aspects in building trust. If I think back to times when I worked with organizations where relationships were unstable or if the interactions were so unpredictable people had to tiptoe through them, tension was high and people were constantly on guard. If you're on guard, that's a sure sign that there isn't any trust. To take that one step further, when your relationships within a team or across a company lack trust, you're unlikely to be so proud of your organization that you'll pick up the gum wrapper. Leaving the gum wrapper on the floor when trust is low might manifest itself by not offering an idea because you're not sure how it will be received, or you choose all your words very carefully in an email so it can't be used against you. Having to concern ourselves with things like these diminish engagement. However, when trust is high and you feel safe and supported by your colleagues, you're more likely to pick up the gum wrapper.

HOW TO DEVELOP BEHAVIORAL EXPECTATIONS

Who participates in developing the Behavioral Expectations will depend on the size of your team or company. On a team, generally everyone participates. In medium-sized and larger organizations, the senior team usually does the work. Some organizations include employees at various levels and try to include representation from all functional areas. You'll need to use your judgment in the makeup of the participants. **There is one rule I'd urge you to follow: only allow those people who have earned the right to participate in developing your Behavioral Expectations.** Those people who have "earned the right to participate" are ones who perform at a high level, are excellent teammates, and are proud to work for the company. When people who don't fit this selection criteria are involved, it minimizes the process, diminishes the result, and can make a mockery of what you are trying to accomplish. This can make things tricky when you are creating Behavioral Expectations on a team so you'll have to use your judgment when deciding who to involve. I worked with one medium-sized company who used a team comprised of employees at all levels and representing all functional areas. The participants were selected based on the criteria I mentioned. It was a joy for me to facilitate the discussion, which was lively, enthusiastic, and rigorous. The result was a set of compelling Behavioral Expectations that were ardently followed.

THE METHOD

After defining what Behavioral Expectations are and the benefit of them, I give two index cards to each attendee and instruct each person to write down what they believe are the two most critical Behavioral Expectations for the organization (only one Behavioral Expectation per card). People are free to write a word, a phrase, a sentence—whatever they feel obliged to write. I have found not forcing people into a format allows for greater creativity. Once I've gathered everyone's responses, I place all the cards face up on a table and ask all the participants to look for patterns. Then, we sort the cards by finding trends and removing the givens. The givens, basic behaviors that everyone should possess to be on the team, are things like integrity or moral standard. We combine the cards that have matching patterns, putting them in like piles and laying those next to any single, outlier cards. For example, all cards that mention "unity" in some form or fashion are put in the same pile. If only one card mentions "continuous learning," that outlier card is its own pile. Because we only want a maximum of five Behavioral Expectations, we prioritize the piles of cards. **This is another key point: most organizations have far too many core values.** (Very few organizations have Behavioral Expectations, that's why I call them core values here.) Before I started to work with one company, they had over fifteen core values! While they were well-intentioned, the list was too overwhelming to be useful. When I randomly asked people who worked for the company what their core values were, over 66 percent responded they didn't even know the core values existed.

We then take a maximum of five and draft a memorable phrase for each one. I instruct leaders not to share these, but instead to personally try to live them over the next month. This is an important step. It's easy to sit around a table and proclaim that we should act in accordance with these, but it's usually harder to live them during the day when you're stressed or dealing with someone you don't particularly enjoy working with. After the pilot period, we come back together to discuss how the month went. I'll ask questions like:

- How did it feel to behave guided by these?
- What struggles did you have?
- Are these realistic?
- Would these be the most important behaviors we'd want all employees to live by?

This discussion can lead to modifying or replacing one or more of the Behavioral Expectations. Being selective and precise with which Behavioral Expectations you choose and how they are worded is important.

Inevitably, the group will say these were harder to carry out than they expected. This is a key point because it shows how difficult it can be to modify our behavior when we're consciously trying. If you've got more people on the team or in the organization who will be required to follow the same guidelines, it's also a precursor to what you'll encounter when you try to get everyone following them; that's where the next stage of real work comes in.

Establishing Behavioral Expectations may take more than one iteration of drafting and more than one month of practice before you take the next step: sharing them with the rest of the people in the organization. If you feel like you need that extra time, take it. It's better to go slow and get it right than to go fast and roll out something that will have little impact.

Once you solidify your Behavioral Expectations, they should be communicated to everyone. You'll want to be clear about why you're instituting these, noting the benefits already mentioned and providing examples of what each Behavioral Expectation looks like in daily life. Some of these examples will come from the pilot period. Others will be more obvious. And some will come as everyone lives them. One company had a Behavioral Expectation of "Being Responsible Makes Us All Comfortable." The team developing the Behavioral Expectations came up with these examples:

- Respond to emails and phone calls within twenty-four hours.
- Only commit to what you can do.
- Take initiative to make the company better.

During the pilot period, one of the leaders realized being responsible also meant "helping others when they were in need." When the Behavioral Expectations were rolled out to every employee, these examples were shared to provide a foundation of how to act in accordance with "Being Responsible Makes Us All Comfortable."

Additionally, complying with the Behavioral Expectations is something everyone will need time to get comfortable with. Rarely does everyone immediately live these. Those who participated in the one-month (or more) pilot, can speak to this. The best communication process I've seen organizations use—and this will depend on the size of your team—is to have the CEO unveil them at an all-team meeting. Immediately following, they send a company-wide email reiterating the CEO's message. Then each leader, beginning with the executive team, meets with her direct reports to reiterate the message from the CEO and discuss why following Behavioral Expectations is important. Then, in a cascading fashion, each leader holds a similar meeting with his team. All leaders beginning with the CEO should communicate this change in a personal and reassuring manner. Within a few months of introducing the Behavioral Expectations, the final step is to embed them as the basis for all your people processes: hiring, firing, promoting, performance appraisal ratings (if you still use them), monthly coaching sessions, and any other people processes that exist in your company.

Here are ways leaders have embedded their Behavioral Expectations:

- One leader redesigned her interview questions to ensure she found people who were naturally drawn to a workplace that ascribed to the Behavioral Expectations her team had created. This leader also fully explained each Behavioral Expectation and their importance at the end of the interview.
- In one organization, a team member consistently

violated the company's Behavioral Expectation of "Everyone Deserves Your Best." Her interactions were described as demeaning, and she was known for giving abrupt and sarcastic answers. People throughout this small company stopped seeking her help. Her manager began to coach her, but the employee couldn't control her frustration when a mistake was made. Unable to comply with this Behavioral Expectation, the employee was terminated even though her performance was fine. This is a good example of where Behavioral Expectations carried the same degree of importance as performance expectations. This one act also signaled that the Behavioral Expectations should be taken seriously.

- On another team, when employees applied for a position, the internal selection process had as one criterion how effectively each employee executed the Behavioral Expectations.

- One organization added their Behavioral Expectations to their performance appraisal. The Behavioral Expectations carried a 50 percent weighting in every employee's evaluation, signaling how important these were in measuring overall performance.

Such actions go a long way to ensure you hire and mold the type of leaders and team members who create stability, predictability, and trust when they work with colleagues.

The success of the Behavioral Expectations taking hold to be an important driver of your culture depends mostly on the modeling, recognizing, and coaching done by the leaders. Bobby is a phenomenal example of what it truly means for a leader to model the Behavioral Expectations. Bobby's company had a Behavioral Expectation of "Company Above Self," meaning, in part, that decisions would be made to create a unified team, even when that decision wasn't in someone's personal best interest. As a leader within the sales team, it is Bobby's job to motivate his team members and produce solid numbers—and, as a well-networked, competitive, high-performing salesperson, he typically does just that. To incentivize the teams to perform, Bobby's company offers an award at every quarterly sales meeting to the top performing team. It's an important event for the company.

Just before a recent meeting, numbers were tallied, and it became clear Bobby's team tied with another sales team in the company. Since Bobby's team had won the previous two quarterly awards, Bobby offered to give the award to the other group—an act of true selflessness. When Bobby relayed his decision to his team members, he also took the time to explain why: he was trying to help create a unified organization where colleagues worked in each other's best interests. He wanted to lead by example. His team appreciated Bobby's big-hearted gesture, but they appreciated the explanation even more because it filled them with pride and inspired them to be good stewards of the company's culture.

MAKE BEHAVIORAL EXPECTATIONS A PRIORITY

The method of developing, communicating, and embedding your Behavioral Expectations takes time. **Most companies unveil their Behavioral Expectations with elaborate fanfare, but after a few months, the gusto is gone and it's back to business as usual.** Embedding Behavioral Expectations is difficult because we may be asking people to change their behavior, and they may not see any need to do that. That's why coaching and recognition are required to modify and align everyone's behavior. In most companies, individual achievement is the pinnacle of success. Hit your performance goals—or better yet, exceed them—and enjoy the financial benefits as your reward. How you behave on the way to that success can be less important. **For Behavioral Expectations to matter, you must make them of equal importance to performance expectations.** That means if a person is on pace to exceed her performance goals but is doing it in a way that violates the Behavioral Expectations, that can't be ok.

In one company I worked with, there was a top performer, Bitsy, who was an absolute terror to work with. She bullied everyone to get what she wanted. She routinely used her position of power to threaten those who resisted her wants. She was also self-serving, political, and divisive. Ironically, one of the Behavioral Expectations for the company was "Be a Team Player." Her actions made a mockery of any serious attempt to make this Behavioral Expectation the guidepost for interactions. If her leader had worked with her to change her approach or, if she couldn't make the shift, terminated her, it would have sent a clear signal to every employee that the Behavioral Expectations were inviolate. Sadly, he sat idly by. As time passed, talented people who interacted with Bitsy on a regular basis began to avoid her. Some only communicated by email so they had a paper trail for protection. One person told his boss he wouldn't work with her unless it was absolutely necessary—ironic outcomes for a company that wanted everyone to "Be a Team Player." **Meeting performance objectives without living Behavioral Expectations should not be a reason to *keep* your job.**

Keeping Behavioral Expectations a priority is a thorough and fragile process that requires consistent energy and effort. It's like growing a flower: if we don't water and fertilize the flower, it will die. If we don't keep Behavioral Expectations top-of-mind with our team, they will die, too. **Excellence takes effort.**

One organization has a Behavioral Expectation of "One

Unified Team." An employee in that company, Jill, is always pitching in and helping others, even when it isn't her responsibility. She'll also volunteer for projects and participate on committees. Occasionally this will mean staying late, but Jill truly believes she needs to be a model for the Behavioral Expectations, and she lives them consistently. Ultimately, her commitment and follow-through substantially increase her influence in the company; she's seen as highly productive and a joy to work with. You can always count on Jill to pick up the gum wrapper and to inspire those around her to do the same. Some of that is Jill's nature, but of equal importance is the well-defined Behavioral Expectations the company has and prioritizes. The other point that's important is that while an employee like Bitsy, if left unchecked, can single-handedly devastate the culture by ignoring the Behavioral Expectations, an employee like Jill can help a positive culture flourish by modeling the Behavioral Expectations.

WAIT, THERE'S MORE...

Here are a few other things companies do to keep their Behavioral Expectations in the forefront of every employee's mind:

- ◆ Review them at every all-team meeting.
- ◆ Start each meeting with a story that illustrates some-

one living a Behavioral Expectation. This takes about two minutes and provides a big bang for your buck because along with demonstrating what a Behavioral Expectation looks like in action, it also recognizes someone on the team as the hero of the story and gets the meeting off to a positive start.

- Begin every week with a morning announcement, taken from the high school activity by the same name, where a company-wide voicemail further clarifies and explains a Behavioral Expectation. These announcements can also mention employee birthdays, happenings during the week, and an inspirational quote.
- Put the Behavioral Expectations on a placard that is placed on everyone's desk.
- Put the Behavioral Expectations on a screen saver on everyone's computer.

All these ideas are designed as reminders, not as substitutes for daily modeling, coaching, and recognizing.

HOW TO INSTILL SELF-ACCOUNTABILITY

As leaders, we need to model the way by living the Behavioral Expectations. Your heart and mind must be filled with their spirit. If not, they have absolutely no chance of gaining traction. We must hold our team accountable, but ideally, we want them to hold *themselves* accountable.

Self-accountability is more effective than manager-mandated accountability. It's better for everyone when our team members willingly do what we need them to do.

Some members of the team will naturally hold themselves accountable when you explain the importance and ask them to. Others? Not as much. For the folks in the "not as much" camp, here is a story I recently read that illustrates an effective approach. A minor league baseball player with major league talent had a bad habit of failing to run hard on ground balls. If the ball he hit looked like an easy out, he half-heartedly jogged to first base—a cardinal sin in baseball. His manager could have taken punitive actions like benching him during the game to send a message, but the manager had a better plan.

The manager brought the player into his office and showed him videos of the player sprinting when he hit a ground ball that was a tough play for an infielder, hustling to stretch a single into a double, and when this player was positioned in the outfield going all out to make a diving catch. The video then showed the player lollygagging down to first on a few routine ground ball outs. After watching the video, the manager asked the player how he thought kids who bought his jersey or had his bobblehead doll would feel when they saw this. What about family members? His teammates? The player recognized the error of his ways; hustling never was an issue again, and the player made it to the major leagues.

The manager's approach was brilliant. With great care and recognition for the player's potential, he impressed upon the young man how his actions impacted others and the reputation he was creating for himself. You can use a similar approach with people on your team who don't immediately adhere to the Behavioral Expectations. Holding people accountable doesn't have to be punitive, even though that is the view most everyone has. Account-ability, following the baseball manager's example, can be developmental and have a positive impact on the person's life. It can be done in a way that makes the person want to be better. **This positive approach solves the problem, keeps the person's self-confidence high, and keeps your relationship on solid footing.** All of these are crit-ical factors in the continued unity and performance of the team.

HOW ABOUT THE HABITUAL VIOLATORS?

On those rare occasions when a team member doesn't respond to our continued coaching, we need to part ways with the employee. Some people are just not a good fit for the culture we're trying to create. Here, understand that we're talking about a habitual violator who makes little effort to change. Even good people who try to do the right thing are going to slip every now and then. We're all human, and we all have bad days. Smart people occasionally do stupid things. That, however, is not the type of person we're talking about.

The employee we need to be wary of is the one who ignores the Behavioral Expectations, makes little effort to comply, or is unable to comply. **We should expect the behaviors we accept.** If we accept bad behavior, it will only continue. **Allowing poor behavior to continue without consequence diminishes our influence as a leader. Conversely, taking decisive action when it is warranted bolsters our influence.** The reality is everyone on a team knows when someone doesn't really care about trying to be a good teammate, and they are looking for us to act.

In one organization, Otto entered as a manager, and there were high hopes for him. He had a large network in the industry that would generate business. He was well-respected in the community which augmented the company's reputation. In what was counter to what he displayed during the interview process, Otto immediately, upon taking the position, created a fear-based environment for his team. He would literally scream at people who didn't do what he wanted them to do. He threatened people. Because of his limited time in the organization, he didn't have many answers to procedural questions, yet he would prevent people on the team from calling other departments for help. Despite an in-depth review of the Behavioral Expectations during the onboarding process followed by intense coaching from his manager, Otto's actions seemed to get worse instead of better. For a company whose Behavioral Expectations were "We are Family" and "Your Friends Work Here," something needed to be done quickly, and it was. Within nine weeks of being hired and being given multiple chances to make corrections, Otto was terminated—an act that reinforced everyone's belief in the company that the Behavioral Expectations guided decisions. The tension created during Otto's tenure took a toll on the number of gum wrappers being picked up. However, because Otto's manager acted swiftly, employees returned to their practice of leaving no gum wrappers around the office.

A TOOL TO MEASURE BEHAVIORAL EXPECTATIONS: THE BE REPORT CARD

In the BE Report Card exercise, the employee self-evaluates his effectiveness in living the Behavioral Expectations. An example of the Report Card, with instructions, is listed in the Appendix. You'll see that the grading system is a simple ABC setup, with an A grade being achieved when the Behavioral Expectation being rated is lived 95 percent of the time. Obviously, 100 percent is what we're after, but we're all human and we get frustrated, angry, and disrespectful from time to time. At 95 percent, we account for those occasional missteps.

As leaders we should have a good handle on how well each of our team members is living the Behavioral Expectations. The second Report Card is for us leaders to evaluate our employee. This should be done independently of the team member completing his Report Card and prior to meeting with him. A key in using this tool is being able to point to examples of this employee putting each Behavioral Expectation into action. That's how we really deepen everyone's understanding of what the Behavioral Expectations look like in real life.

When meeting with the employee, swap cards, and read the other's evaluation. It's always interesting to see how much agreement exists. If there is a lack of agreement, that's probably the first thing to discuss. If there are any Bs or Cs, that would be the next thing to discuss. Don't forget to discuss the As! Many times, we can get caught up in what's not working. Be careful to avoid the trap; most people have As on their Report Card and we want to recognize those.

This tool keeps the conversation, and a sense of the priority, alive. If you have routine meetings with each of your team members—I recommend monthly—you want to have the Report Card on the agenda continuously. If you see the Behavioral Expectations are taking hold with an employee, you can back off to a quarterly conversation, but I wouldn't go much past that.

If you're an executive leader meeting with senior leaders, this might seem too elementary; another trap to avoid. It's most important that you are taking an honest account of your team members. After all, you have the most influence in the company. If you carry this out and set the expectation that the Report Card cascades through the company, everyone will participate. Ultimately, your Behavioral Expectations will set the standard for the way people conduct themselves in the company. **Exemplary conduct is driven by devotion to the Behavioral Expectations.**

A SYMBIOTIC RELATIONSHIP

Now, we've looked at two of our three steps in the overall process: CliftonStrengths, combined with effectively applied Behavioral Expectations, gives us a complementary balance of acceptance and appreciation for each person while everyone follows the same standards of behavior. No more condescending conversations, end runs, or interactions where someone is left feeling attacked—a dynamic that leads to higher levels of trust and greater self-esteem, while allowing everyone to use their natural talent themes to thrive.

That's not the end of the story, though. The lubricant that makes this work are the Leadership Practices. **Leadership is the make or break factor in a company.** The leader sets direction, guides strategy and influences the team. Accordingly, leaders have a heavier mantle. **One of the best questions a leader can ask herself is: Would people follow me if I didn't have the title?** Position power is of little value in today's workplace. Just because someone has the title doesn't mean he's a leader. I once worked with a man who took over a management position and, in his initial meeting with his team, said, "You don't have to respect me, but you will respect my title." **Demanding respect is rarely the way you get it.** Despite my ongoing coaching, the manager refused to change his mindset. After a few months, his team rebelled at his controlling ways, and he was terminated. No one followed him even when he had the title! People will follow leaders they trust and who invest in them. This is the result of implementing the five Leadership Practices that follow. Deliver on these Leadership Practices, and you will guide people to becoming the best editions of themselves. Along the way you'll be at your best, too.

Using each practice fortifies an environment of commitment, one where everyone picks up the gum wrapper. The first of those practices might seem a little fluffy, but don't be fooled. An investment in helping a person discover her purpose at work is a good starting point because you can learn what's important to her. It's a motivational driver that dovetails with our first two steps and opens the door to the rest of the Leadership Practices.

BUILD DEFINED LEADERSHIP PRACTICES

CHAPTER 5

————

GOT PURPOSE?

One question that usually gets asked around the dinner table is, "How was work?" That question and ensuing discussion are part of just about everyone's evening. It points to another question: **What do you want people to say about you? That might be the most important question we ever ask ourselves as leaders.** That question doesn't suggest we need to make decisions based on what every employee wants when those wants don't help meet goals or aren't in the best interest of the team or the organization. It's more about leading in a way that creates a positive environment. That can be a tall task, but we have more influence to make that a reality than we realize. As leaders, we have the power to alter people's lives. I was the beneficiary of such a leader.

My first "real job" was in loss prevention at a bank, which meant I was involved in tracking down anyone who wrote a bad check or overdrew their account. While there were aspects of the job I enjoyed, the lion's share of the position came with built-in confrontation and unending negativity—counter to who I am as a person. People describe me as upbeat, self-motivated, and enthusiastic, but those natural characteristics were worn down by the daily struggle of working in a job that didn't match my talent themes. At the end of every weekend, I'd get the Sunday Night Blues. I hated my job and cringed at the thought of heading to the office on Monday morning. **When you dread Sunday night, your job's not right.**

The manager from the bank's Training Department, Maria, noticed I did a good job when I conducted check fraud training for newly hired tellers. Maria also noticed my development was at a standstill, and recommended I join her team. I jumped at the opportunity. The position was much more suited to my talents; and when I was able to better align my strengths with my job duties, it changed everything. I realized work didn't have to be something you disliked. It could be a place for self-expression and collaboration. My Sunday night dread transformed into anticipation for Monday. **I did—and still do—*get* to go to work, not *have* to go to work.**

I'm so thankful to Maria for investing in me. She holds a special place in my heart for the dramatic improvement she brought to my life by spotting my strengths, aligning them with my work, and giving me consistent feedback and coaching.

The lesson Maria taught me in our years working together is that when a manager is focused on her employees, sees the potential in them, invests in them, and believes in them, it provides a springboard for the employees' performance to soar and to live better lives. Working for Maria changed my nightly dinner conversations.

At the heart of Maria's actions was her goal to understand what made work meaningful for me. When we'd meet each month to discuss my development, Maria, would ask me questions like, "Why do you come to work every morning at this bank in this job?" "What legacy do you want to leave?" "What do you want people to say about you in this company?" "How do you want to feel about the contribution you make to your colleagues?"

I was in my late twenties, and no one had ever asked me those questions. I never thought about why I went to work other than to make money; I'd always been taught a job was a means to an end. You needed work to fund your lifestyle, and it never occurred to me that work could be more than that. But these conversations with Maria shifted my perspective which, in turn, powered my performance. The work itself could have meaning. There was purpose beyond a paycheck. For me, the meaning of work comes from making a positive impact in people's lives. Maria helped me realize that we all need a purpose at work. That purpose can fuel us every day. It can make those rough days more palatable because we can take the longer view.

We can do for our team members what Maria did for me—and what many leaders I've worked with have done for their employees. Asking questions of people like Maria asked of me can start the conversation. Know that this may be a discussion that takes thought and time. It's one to be slow played rather than expecting an immediate answer.

Here's another example of how this worked with one leader and a person on her team: the leader asked the employee, Delaney, what drove her to get up in the morning and come to work. At first, Delaney didn't have an answer other than for a paycheck and health insurance, but her manager didn't settle for that answer. She knew there was more to it than that. Delaney was a top performer and a wonderful teammate. She was the type of employee any company would fight to keep. Over a series of meetings, her manager kept asking Delaney questions like, "What's missing in your job today that if we could add it would be a motivator for you?" and, "What in your job gives you the feeling that you're making a difference?"

Over a couple of months, Delaney began to think more

deeply about her purpose for working. She always went out of her way to help people improve. Even though this wasn't part of her official job description, she was a natural teacher, patient and understanding in those times when she was assisting anyone in her company. Tying the idea of having a purpose to Delaney's CliftonStrengths Profile, Delaney had Developer and Empathy at the top of her profile. [People exceptionally talented in the Developer theme recognize and cultivate the potential in others. They spot the signs of each small improvement and derive satisfaction from evidence of progress.] [People exceptionally talented in the Empathy theme can sense other people's feelings by imagining themselves in others' lives or situations.]

Delaney began to see her purpose as "being a coach as much as a doer." Her manager encouraged her to spend time informally coaching others and kept on the lookout for opportunities to send people Delaney's way, but it didn't stop there. Delaney's manager asked her if she would have an interest in spearheading the company's community involvement effort. Delaney's manager knew that Delaney liked to work with young people in need. Delaney jumped at the opportunity, which further motivated her. Delaney is not only a star performer, but she is a star performer who is even more engaged in her job, solidly committed to her manager and less likely to leave for more money. Delaney has told me that when she tells her husband about her day at work, she talks about it with enthusiasm. She also speaks glowingly about her manager, who cared enough to help Delaney discover and cultivate her purpose.

To get started, you need to understand your own purpose. If you've never thought about this, it may take some introspection. Allow yourself the thinking time. While it may be elusive, it's worth the search. As I mentioned, I never gave something like this a thought until I worked with Maria. While she didn't specifically label our discussions as "determining your purpose," my end result—making a positive impact in people's lives—became my guidepost which I used to direct my actions and decisions. It has served me well in my career because it's naturally who I am, and it's what I truly believe I should do for other people. When you know why you're getting up in the morning, work becomes more invigorating. When you act in accordance with your purpose, you can create a legacy that will last beyond you. **That's what great leaders do: create something meaningful that outlives them.**

Here are some questions you can use to start your thinking:

* Why do you come to work every day?
* What do you want more of in your job?
* What is the most important contribution you can make in the lives of people who report to you?

- What do you want to be known for at work?
- Is there something in your job that is missing that, if you added it to your role, would create more meaning for you?
- What impact do you want to have?
- Why do you do a good job when you do a good job?
- Why do you go above and beyond when there is no recognition?
- What work would you go above and beyond for if nothing was attributed to you?

Here are how some people have described their purpose:

- To promote kindness
- To achieve great things with friends
- To build the most admired company in our industry
- To help my colleagues achieve their goals
- To move people toward success in their careers
- To outperform everyone I compete against
- To provide the best life for my family
- To be top in my field

As you can see, one's purpose is specific to her. The key is to discover what is important to you and then make it a reality every day. As leaders, we can also facilitate this for others. Asking team members to answer questions like those listed and offering your help as a sounding board is invaluable. **People have more to offer than the job they**

do. Think about how you can help your team members live out their purpose. Most people want to be associated with something bigger than their daily work. We've probably all had a job at one time in our lives that didn't fit our strengths, challenge us, or allow us to achieve our greater purpose. That's a hollow feeling. Having purpose is about recognizing and reversing that trajectory in those we're given the privilege to lead. I've lived this. Moving to work that was compatible with my talent themes was the first step. Once I had that congruence, I was unencumbered by the weight of just getting through each day that a bad job fit saddles us with. This allowed me to take the next step of finding my purpose to make each day meaningful.

CHAPTER 6

MANAGE TO OUTCOMES

I once worked with a manager who was upset because he felt one of his employees spent too much time having personal conversations on the phone with her daughter during work hours. These weren't the kind of check-in calls that every parent has during the workday. They were long, casual calls that weren't urgent.

"Does she meet her goals?" I asked.

"Well, yes," he replied. "She produces quality work. I don't have any complaints other than the phone issue."

"If she's performing well and the phone calls aren't interrupting her productivity or the departments, maybe she just doesn't have enough to do," I said.

He paused.

"Maybe you're right," he answered. "But shouldn't she try to do more on her own?"

"Yes," I said. "But if her tendency is not to seek out work, you need to take the reins and lead her in a positive way. Let's look at her CliftonStrengths Profile and see what that tells us in conjunction with what you know about her."

As we reviewed her Strengths Profile, it became evident that she was far better at reacting than initiating. Once she was given something to do, she did it well. Upon reflection, this matched what her manager saw in her performance every day. The manager realized that his employee was likely waiting for her next assignment, and, until she received it, felt she had time to do other things like chat with her daughter. He realized that he needed to be more proactive in distributing work.

You might be thinking, "C'mon, she needs to take responsibility and ask for more work. That's what she gets paid for." A fair point, but when you really start to know the people on your team, you lead them in a way that works for them. This way ensures they do quality work and fosters commitment. It also reduces everyone's frustration. When I say, "know the people on your team," I mean know their talents and strengths as much as you know what they did over the weekend. Don't get me wrong; building intimacy with people by knowing things about their personal lives is important to your long-term relationship, and you want to do that. Coupling this with knowing people's talents and needs builds a deeper level of knowledge that, when properly utilized, will pay significant dividends.

GIVE YOUR TEAM THE FREEDOM TO BE THEMSELVES

It's more effective to work with people as they are than to try to change them to suit our needs. I'm not talking about the need to modify someone's behavior to match the Behavioral Expectations, which is a must. I'm referring to figuring out how to get the most from each person as they are. Everyone will be better for it. Performance will be better, too. In the prior example, if the manager had forced the employee to come to him each time she completed one assignment so he could give her another, that would have been difficult for her to maintain because it was against her nature. Knowing her strengths, he set up a queue so assignments automatically filtered to her and she could respond to them. This improved her production and reduced his frustration. The more a person can use her reservoir of natural talent to complete the work, the more effective she'll be. Additionally, most people crave autonomy. A light touch is usually welcomed. Even in the prior example, once the manager recognized how to effectively lead his employee by providing a pipeline of work to be done, he let her accomplish the work in her own way. The quality she produced was never in question. The caveat here, though, is when someone is new to the role or has a new responsibility. Obviously, more direct instruction will be needed.

Know that instruction doesn't mean forcing people to do the job the way you would do it. **Force kills individuality.** You have to allow people freedom to achieve their objectives in the way they work most naturally. That's why it's critical to have very clear performance expectations in place and then manage to those outcomes, allowing each person the independence to accomplish those expectations using the distinct nature of his strengths. You're not abandoning the person; you're there to support and advise when needed.

I used to work with Ryan, an accounting department manager. If he had a project due on a Friday, Ryan worked on it a little at a time throughout the week until it was finished. One of Ryan's employees, Dominique, often found herself with similar projects. She'd start her part of the departmental report on Friday morning and turn it in on Friday afternoon. Ryan was frustrated; he wanted her to perform on his timeline because that's how he worked most comfortably. Dominique, however, truly worked best when she was prompted by the pressure to meet a deadline. She excelled under the compressed timeline. Ryan thought Dominque was procrastinating, and Dominique thought Ryan's management of her was stifling and unreasonable. Along with the hard feelings this caused in their relationship, Ryan's demands hampered Dominque's performance.

Once Ryan realized this by comparing the dominant talent themes in his CliftonStrengths Assessment to Dominque's, he began to accept her style even though it was counter to his. As they talked through their differences, a lightning bolt struck Ryan: Dominique's way of working wasn't born out of putting things off or laziness but of a compulsion to perform at a high level in her own way. After all, she produced the required results on time. As they talked, Dominique's desire to produce excellence was evident. Dominique gave Ryan feedback about the way he managed her, and she asked for more freedom to complete the work as she saw fit. Ryan agreed. He focused his energy on managing the outcome that was agreed upon. The relationship was mended in large part by Ryan's new style of leadership. Dominque continued to turn in top-notch work on time, and Ryan was grateful for the quality of her results.

THE DIFFICULTY IN DEFINING GOALS

We want people to be free to accomplish their work

in their way so they achieve their goals. There is a business to run, and we need everyone to achieve their goals for it to be successful. According to research conducted by Gallup, about half of working adults in the US are unclear about what they are supposed to do at work. Additionally, only 3 percent of employees report having a review of their performance monthly.[7] The implications of that are frightening! First, employees don't know what to do—then they get no feedback! That's like trying to get through a maze by yourself with a blindfold on. It's more difficult than it should be.

Based on my research, there are three reasons for this dilemma. The first one, and usually the least common, is that managers and employees don't set measurable goals. Typically in sales functions, it's easier to set measurable goals because there are numbers to hit. In a function like training and development, goals might be more difficult to quantify. If the goals lack specificity and measurement, an employee knows he's going in the right direction but not sure when achieving the goal will be a direct hit.

A second reason, and a more common one, is that priorities change. If we started the year with a set of goals but the business needs shift, what was once important to achieve is no longer as imperative. If conversations are

---

7   Gallup. "Re-Engineering Performance Management." Gallup.com. Accessed April 16, 2019.
     https://www.gallup.com/workplace/238064/re-engineering-performance-management.aspx.

not dedicated to reviewing and altering the original goals, then confusion occurs. This happens frequently because most managers not only have to lead a team but also carry a significant workload and goals of their own. That workload has managers trying to accomplish their own goals first and foremost and managing their team second. That's understandable with the pace most managers have to keep to get their own work done. Unfortunately, the unintended consequence of this can be delayed communication about changing goals or missed opportunities to observe a team member in action to offer feedback. This problem is exacerbated by the fact that some managers find it easier to get their work done than to have discussions about changing goals or providing feedback.

The third and most common reason for the lack of direction and feedback is that there are competing demands. In many workplaces, everything we are expected to do is urgent. Just about every piece of work is stamped "ASAP." In others, employees work in a matrixed environment and are getting work delegated from multiple sources. Only 26 percent of employees say their manager effectively helps them prioritize their work.[8] All of these things conspire to create uncertainty for employees about what to work on.

---

8   Gallup. "Re-Engineering Performance Management." Gallup.com. Accessed April 16, 2019.
    https://www.gallup.com/workplace/238064/re-engineering-performance-management.aspx.

A PERFORMANCE GOAL SETTING REMEDY: ASK

One way to offset some of these obstacles is to follow the acronym ASK when setting performance goals. **ASK stands for Agreed-upon, Strengths-based, and Known.** Agreed-upon means setting goals that are mutually determined. Some organizations cascade goals downward based on the strategic plan. The plan is usually determined by the board and the executive team. Once the plan is solidified, each division is given their goals in order to hit the plan, and those goals cascade through the company. It makes sense, except that it usually doesn't involve all people who have to achieve the goals. **Involvement is critical to goal achievement.** In my experience, goals are much more effective when they intersect with the interests and talents of the people who need to accomplish them. As leaders, including our team members in the development of their goals creates more ownership. It can be easier for someone to excuse away a goal that was forced upon them versus one in which they were part of the development. Even if goals are given to us as leaders, we likely have latitude in how we distribute those performance goals. That should be done in collaboration with our team members with an eye toward matching goals to each person's strengths. The same applies for goals that we as leaders create. Collaborating on goals might take longer to develop, but the increased desire to execute them is worth that investment. Typically, the more experienced the person, the more input she should have. This might seem radical to some, but delegating the development of goals to experienced, high-performing team members makes good sense. Who knows better what she can accomplish than the performer herself? It's always a judgment call, but that's a trust-building action like no other because **ownership results when my thoughts are included. Disinterest occurs when thoughts are dictated to me.**

It's important that performance goals be Strengths-based. If you've been having discussions with each member of the team about her strengths, you have an idea of what she is best at and enjoys. As much as possible, you want her goals to focus on those strengths for two key reasons, and the first is rooted in performance. When each of us is working from our talents and strengths, our results will be exponentially better than if we are working from a deficit position or a weakness. The second is centered on commitment. It's always more enjoyable to spend time on the work you're good at and enjoy than on the work you're good at but don't care about (or worse yet, the work that drains you of energy because you find it boring or you're uncomfortable with your performance). **Give people work that will feed their minds and inspire their hearts.** Strengths-based work has that power. Think back to the countless examples you've read in previous pages; when strengths are at the core of the work someone does, joy and energy are boundless. The other benefit: **weaknesses are made inconsequential.** What better place to work than one where you are rarely asked to complete tasks that steal your vitality? A place where you are rarely asked to work on something you have to slough through because you don't have the natural talent to perform it excellently?

Here is a tool that will complement the CliftonStrengths work you have been doing with your team members. I call this two-by-two grid the Strengths Matrix, a copy of which has also been included in the Appendix for easy access.

STRENGTHS (GREAT AT/LOVE IT)	POSSIBLE STRENGTHS (NOT GOOD AT YET/ENJOY IT)
LEARNED (GOOD AT/ DON'T ENJOY IT)	WEAKNESSES (NOT GOOD AT/DON'T ENJOY IT)

In the upper left-hand corner is the box for Strengths. As I've mentioned, strengths in this context are those tasks, activities, responsibilities, etc. that the person is good at and enjoys. In my work with individuals, this quadrant is moderately populated. That's not to say people on your team won't place the majority of their work here. I wanted to share my experience so discouragement doesn't creep in if this quadrant doesn't have much written in it. In the upper right-hand corner are Possible Strengths. These are tasks or activities that a person might enjoy but isn't good at yet because they haven't had enough experience. This quadrant represents work people have dabbled in or experimented with and is usually very lightly populated. **We want to point people in the direction of their Strengths; we don't want to cap people. Our talents have a wide array of applicability, and we want people to stretch the limits of that applicability.**

As an example, in a small manufacturing company I worked with, Chaley, a mechanic thought he could assist the sales force by answering customers' questions. Chaley's knowledge of the equipment was exceptional, and he felt he could use his expertise to benefit the company when a prospect or customer raised a question that was too technical for a member of the sales team. While the owner of the company had some reservations worrying that Chaley would be pulled away from his day job, he agreed to have Chaley take calls on a trial basis. The plan worked well. Because Chaley only fielded the most challenging questions, he was still able to work on the equipment as scheduled. The sales reps appreciated the added support and saw their acquisition and retention numbers climb. In turn, Chaley enjoyed the interaction with customers and prospects, which added to his commitment level. Chaley's Possible Strength became a Strength as he gained experience. He also picked up more gum wrappers.

Of course, not all Possible Strengths become Strengths. For instance, take Marybeth, an experienced trainer at a financial services company. Marybeth loved classroom facilitation, which was a strength of hers, but she wanted to try her hand at instructional design. This was something she hadn't done before, but she did have knowledge of program design. Marybeth's manager gave her a small design project to work on, and the finished product was good. Marybeth liked the variety the design work offered. Soon after, another, more time-consuming project came along for which Marybeth volunteered. This time Marybeth found herself staggering to the finish line. Her finished project was average. It lacked the attention to detail and flair with which Marybeth delivered programs in the classroom. When she and her manager debriefed, Marybeth commented that the extended design work was draining. Her top talent themes were Communication, Includer, and WOO. [People exceptionally talented in the Communication theme generally find it easy to put their thoughts into words. They are good conversationalists and presenters.] [People exceptionally talented in the Includer theme accept others. They show awareness of those who feel left out and make an effort to include them.] [People exceptionally talented in the WOO theme love the challenge of meeting new people and winning them over. They derive satisfaction from breaking the ice and making connection with someone.] These made her terrific in the front of the room but were lost while she was in the isolated, process-driven world of program design. It became obvious to Marybeth and her manager that instructional design wasn't a Strength of hers.

The idea of exploring Possible Strengths is to determine if members of the team can broaden their contribution by doing more of the things they're good at and enjoy.

In the bottom left-hand corner of the matrix are Learned Activities. These are tasks, activities, and responsibilities we're good at but don't derive any energy from. They are usually tasks we have to perform as part of our job, but if we stopped doing them tomorrow, that would be fine. Most people heavily fill this quadrant which typically signifies that work isn't challenging or inspiring—it's drudgery. **We all get really good at things we don't enjoy. We do them because we have to not because we want to.** The biggest mistake we can make as leaders is seeing someone who is good at something and assume that's a strength. Remember, the hallmark of a strength is the energy the activity brings. Our biggest opportunity for increasing performance and improving people's lives is to collaborate with people to move items out of this quadrant and replace them with ones that fit into the Strengths quadrant.

In the bottom right-hand quadrant are Weaknesses. These are tasks, activities, and responsibilities where we don't feel comfortable with our results and that drain us of energy. The major difference between Weaknesses and Learned Activities is that Weaknesses are things we aren't good at. We usually "don't mind" performing Learned Activities, but with Weaknesses there's discomfort. Too much time spent here is debilitating. In the previous example with Marybeth and the instructional design process, Marybeth categorized design as a Weakness because she was uncomfortable with her results and it drained her of "every last drop of energy" she had to complete it. This quadrant is usually lightly populated because if a person is spending too much time here, the job isn't a good fit. One point to keep in mind: we need to distinguish a true Weakness from something that needs to be practiced more frequently. Marybeth struggled because her talent themes didn't fit the task, so even if she practiced more, the assignment would have moved to a Learned Activity at best. If someone lists an activity as a Weakness, have conversations about it. It might be that person is at the low end of the learning curve and just needs more practice, or it might be that the activity will always stay in the bottom half of the matrix.

Your goal using this tool is to help every member of your team live above the horizontal line. Once each person completes the Strengths Matrix, discuss it during a monthly 1:1 to determine how, together, you can make shifts so the employee can spend more time at the top half of the grid. To get there for every member of the team, you'll likely have to involve the entire team in an exercise of shifting and trading activities. Don't let job descriptions and role definition constrain you. Most people don't even know what their job description says. For those who do, only 41 percent say that it aligns well with the work they do.[9] Forget conventionality—it's gotten us to a workplace littered with gum wrappers. This exercise can help us determine how we can make goals Strengths-based. We may not be able to make every goal Strengths-based, but the more we can, the more success each team member will have and the more committed each will be—the definition of a kitchen-clean hallway with no gum wrappers.

All the performance goals in the world are meaningless if people lose sight of them as competing demands and changing priorities descend upon them, which is where

9   Gallup. "Re-Engineering Performance Management." Gallup.com. Accessed April 16, 2019.
     https://www.gallup.com/workplace/238064/re-engineering-performance-management.aspx.

the "Known" part of the ASK acronym comes into play. Make your goals measurable and deadline-driven. Each goal must be crystal clear. Once you establish the goals, this shouldn't be a one and done activity. As mentioned, in the course of a year, most of us are faced with competing demands and changing priorities. This becomes a problem in achieving goals that were established months ago. Business isn't typically static, so constant communication around priorities is critical. Some of the highest performing teams I work with have daily stand-up meetings that last fifteen minutes to clarify priorities and determine who's working on what project. In addition to communicating regularly on goals, offer positive and constructive feedback to help our team members improve individually and collectively. Positive feedback is rarely an issue for the person receiving it. Constructive feedback can be different. When given in an environment full of trust, constructive feedback stimulates performance and enhances a sense of teamwork. That said, positive feedback should far outweigh constructive feedback as it boosts self-esteem.

Teamwork is about properly leveraging the gifts of each individual and people supporting one another in the pursuit of excellence. If the feedback feels supportive, it's more likely to be received well. Remember, too, that just because we're supervisors doesn't mean we have "super vision." Give constructive feedback, but ask questions first. Most competent people have a good reason for doing what they do and why they do it. Top performers crave freedom, so be sure to allow people to do the work in a way that works for them.

When it comes to performance goals, keeping people focused on their goals, helping them navigate changing priorities and offering constructive feedback where appropriate will keep everyone's goals Known.

Such proactive leadership, however, is more difficult than it sounds. You probably have other roles in the company besides leading your teams. For example, perhaps you run the accounting department but also have managerial accounting tasks that monopolize most of your time. The cold reality is that letting the leadership side of your job slip is not nearly as limiting to your career as letting the accounting tasks slide. Don't let it happen. People are counting on you. Leadership cannot become an afterthought regardless of your workload. Leadership should be the most important part of your job. If it's not, your team and your entire organization will suffer. **Your impact as a leader is mightier than your role as an individual contributor**.

PERFORMANCE GOALS AND BEHAVIORAL EXPECTATIONS MUST BE OF EQUAL IMPORTANCE

It's important to reiterate that Behavioral Expectations must carry equal weight as a person's performance goals. I'd go so far as to say on a performance appraisal each would be weighted equally because the Behavioral Expectations are driving the culture. If the culture is toxic, performance suffers. Performance rarely suffers in a healthy culture. Using the ASK format, performance goals will be meaningful to team members primarily because the goals will be grounded in each person's Strengths. Blending strengths-based goals with your Behavioral Expectations presents a message that says, "This pairing is how we create a thriving company culture where people who enjoy their work are productive and will always pick up the gum wrappers."

We can't simply *say* both performance goals and Behavioral Expectations are equal; we have to live it. When we do, people notice—and when we don't, they notice even more. Trouble brews when performance goals supersede Behavioral Expectations. Robby, a top performer, worked for a client of mine. Although he put up impressive numbers and excelled at saving clients who were talking about changing providers, Robby completely ignored the Behavioral Expectations and with it the culture the company was trying to create. He was rude to colleagues when he needed something for a customer.

He made promises to customers he couldn't keep simply to boost his sales, then he put undue pressure on others in the company to fulfill nearly impossible delivery demands. If they couldn't get it done, he would blame them and complain to his boss and theirs. In addition, he'd even complain about his coworkers to customers when he couldn't deliver on the promise he had made, even though the promise was unrealistic in the first place.

Unfortunately, Robby's manager didn't think she could afford to fire Robby due to his high productivity. As a result, the carefully created Behavioral Expectations imploded, and the ripple effect of the blast spread to others. Sour attitudes prevailed, as team members throughout the firm became cynical witnessing that the espoused Behavioral Expectations didn't match reality. Trust was lost, the firm's overall performance suffered, and gum wrappers were strewn throughout.

SETTING THE TONE FOR RELENTLESS ACCOMPLISHMENT

In every organization, leaders should set the pace. There's a right way to drive our team to higher levels of performance and there's a wrong way. To me, the right way is modeled by Alexandra, a leader at an organization I work with. She loves her job and works constantly—that's simply how she's wired. She thinks nothing of sending an email from her phone in the middle of the night or leaving a team member a voicemail on their office line at 7:00 p.m. when they're home finishing dinner with their family. Alexandra's messages are always upbeat and supportive. Alexandra manages her life so she feels fulfilled and happy. She wants that for everyone on her team, so she doesn't expect a response at these off times; in fact, she is clear that's not the expectation. Alexandra not only acknowledges there are boundaries, but harps on everyone not to put in the hours she does when it's not needed. There are always seasons when long hours are required to meet a deadline. In those instances, Alexandra makes sure the person logging extra hours isn't feeling overworked or ignoring other aspects of his life. If the person is feeling that way, she figures out ways to mitigate the hours by getting extra help or pitching in herself. Through these actions, Alexandra is conveying that she will do all it takes to perform at the highest level, and she does it with a smile. Alexandra's commitment sets the pace, which positively impacts her team's overall performance. They see her effort and want to match it.

This is in stark contrast to a small business owner I know. He works twenty-four hours a day, seven days a week, and he expects the people in his company to do the same. He can call you at 7:30 AM on a Sunday morning or at 9:00 PM on a Friday night, and his expectation is that you will answer. He calls with a snarl because there is usually a problem. He has no boundaries. Whereas Alexandra's approach sets the tone for her team to do more, the small business owner's approach sets the tone for his employees to quit.

MANAGING TO OUTCOMES: BALANCING FREEDOM AND FOLLOW-UP

People need cultivators, not critics. That's what managing to outcomes is all about. Allowing people to achieve their goals using their preferred methods, supporting their needs, encouraging their progress, offering feedback to help them course-correct and maintaining accountability for results and alignment to the Behavioral Expectations.

Think about all the tasks your employees manage besides their duties at work. They captain their households, perform as family caregivers, coach Little League baseball teams, lead Girl Scout Troops, teach Sunday School, work a side hustle, or any host of other out-of-office activities. Our team members are self-monitoring adults outside of the office. Work can be the one place people lose their freedom; prevent that. **If you believe people will come through, and they know that *you* believe that, they will.**

This might sound like I'm sending conflicting messages,

but realize that freedom does not mean abandonment. **The most successful managers lead with a light touch, not an invisible hand.** They're attentive to their team members. Many managers lead by benign neglect. This usually stems from a fear of not wanting to be seen as a micromanager. Some managers feel that too many status conversations about a project or task can seem smothering, so they avoid having any significant discussions with their team members about performance until there is a problem. By then it can be too late. This is counter to what we've already mentioned when it comes to feedback, but it's a nagging problem for many leaders. It's well-intentioned but ineffective.

One thing I have found to offset undermanagement is to schedule one-on-ones each month. I suggest setting these up as a recurring calendar appointment so you are holding them like clockwork every month irrespective of what else is going on. There are typically six topics that are being discussed:

+ Whatever the team member wants to cover
+ Use of talents and strengths
+ Performance as it relates to goal achievement
+ Motivation
+ Development opportunities
+ Living the Behavioral Expectations

This sets a framework for the agenda that makes the meeting effective and consistent. The design elevates openness and trust.

Later in this chapter, you'll find a coaching guide with questions you can use as discussion starters for this monthly 1:1 meeting. I wouldn't use every question in every meeting, but sprinkle one or two in each meeting. You do want to make sure you have an agenda. A common mistake occurs when a manager tells an employee "Let's start meeting every month so we can stay on top of things. This is your meeting so whatever you want to discuss is on the table." Then the manager does nothing to prepare for the meeting. Most employees don't understand the purpose or feel like everything is ok, so they aren't sure how or what to prepare. The meetings devolve into a "nonversation" where little gets accomplished. Seeing no benefit, the meetings eventually get scuttled. We're the leaders so we need to make sure there is a meaningful agenda adding value for both of us. Even if everything is cruising along, we should use the meetings as a platform for how to more effectively accomplish the six agenda items. That signals a standard of relentless improvement.

The absolute, without a doubt, worst thing you can do is blow off these meetings. Of course, there will be an occasion when something comes up, but reschedule. I can tell you from having done this with countless companies, when you frequently cancel the meeting, it sends a message to your employees that they are not as important as other things you have to do. That message is inherently demoralizing.

WHEN MANAGING TO OUTCOMES DOESN'T GO AS PLANNED

Managing to outcomes doesn't always go as planned. No matter your effort, sometimes people aren't a fit, and it's still our job to do right by them. Consider the example of Barbara, a recently hired credit union teller who was gregarious, positive, and charming—but she couldn't make change. Her teller drawer was short almost every night. In a credit union, when one teller is short, other employees spend time looking for that difference. Barbara's colleagues were staying late at work, frustrated and searching for the incorrect transactions. Barbara's manager recognized her new teller wasn't working out, but she also recognized Barbara's strengths: she had unmatched recall of previous conversations and was extremely welcoming. Barbara easily put members (i.e., customers) at ease and quickly got to know new ones quickly. The manager used her network to find Barbara a sales job where she could use her personality to connect with people but didn't have to work with numbers. The result? Barbara became highly successful in her new role because it played more to who she was as a person and leveraged her natural gifts. And, equally important, she was happy to go to work again instead of feeling like a burden to her colleagues. An unintended payoff for the credit union came when Barbara connected with people she felt might be a good match for her former manager's team. Barbara was quick to refer them, which grew the manager's pool of potential candidates.

Helping an underperforming employee find another position isn't crazy. It's a distinct pattern woven throughout this book: servant leadership. Just because someone isn't good at the same things I am doesn't mean they're not valuable and don't deserve to be happy. Being a servant leader means continually asking ourselves a key question: "How does a person become better off because they work with me?" As a servant leader, we keep people's interests above our own. We don't give up on people. We care for people and consider leading them not only as an opportunity, but as an obligation to make their lives better. Leadership comes with a heavy mantle, and when done well, there are no gum wrappers lying around.

ACTIONABLE TOOLS FOR YOUR ORGANIZATION

Managing to outcomes and creating a trusting, feedback-oriented, positive work environment can seem daunting, but it doesn't have to be. Let's explore two tools you can use to do just that.

MONTHLY CHECK-INS

Meet one-on-one with your team members monthly to gauge the answers to vital questions concerning engagement, including, "How can we optimize the use of your strengths?" and "What do you expect of me?" For a full agenda and list of questions, refer to the 1:1 Coaching Guide in the Appendix. Remember that before each 1:1, be sure to study the employees' CliftonStrengths Assessment results and the Strengths Matrix.

There needs to be a current of authenticity and vulnerability that should run through these meetings. Your goal is to ensure each person on your team shines, and candid conversation is the way to get there.

TEAM MEETINGS

Similar to an earlier example, many managers will say, "I don't need team meetings. I talk to my people every day." My experience tells me that the teams who meet regularly with an agenda are more cohesive and typically higher performing than teams that don't. On these teams, members have input into the agenda. It's our job as managers to set the tone of the meeting—but we don't have to lead every one. Instead, rotate who has control over the meeting. Let team members set the agenda and lead the meeting. When it's your turn to facilitate the meeting, set the example by soliciting feedback from the team when creating the agenda. These small actions send the message that leadership is circular and that every employee is part of the team.

There are other benefits to rotate meeting facilitation:

- It can serve as a development opportunity for some team members.
- When an employee is leading the meeting and isn't getting responses from his colleagues, he may suddenly understand how it feels when he isn't participating.
- As a leader, you can gain a new perspective on the meeting when you're a participant.

Please refer to One-Hour Team Meeting Agenda in the Appendix for a sample itinerary.

CHAPTER 7

ACT WITH BENEVOLENCE

Benevolence means having a disposition to do good. For someone who has a major impact on the lives of others, what better spirit is there with which to lead? Leveraging people's strengths, accepting and appreciating people for who they are, and allowing people to achieve their goals in the way that best suits them are all acts of benevolence. Couple that with living the Behavioral Expectations—the anchor points for individual and collective behaviors at work—and you build a high level of trust within your team. Trust is critical in the workplace because team members need to feel safe and empowered to reveal who they truly are, as well as to take even the most minor risk. **You can always press people to speak up, but they won't say what they're really thinking unless they feel safe.**

EJ, for example, is a leader who acts with benevolence. He has taken the time to study the CliftonStrengths results of each member of his team. This allows him to recognize their individual needs. For instance, he knows that Laz has Competition as a dominant talent. [People who are exceptionally talented in the Competition theme measure their progress against the performance of others. They strive to win first place and revel in contests.] Therefore, Laz is motivated by measuring himself against something or someone. EJ leads a team in the Operations Division of a credit union, so he and Laz play a game of, "Can You Top This?" Every week, Laz has to process a number of incoming wire transfers that beats his total from the last week, while maintaining a zero error rate and following all procedures.

While other team members might see this game as unwanted pressure at best and manipulative at worst, Laz is driven by it. He would likely play the game in his own mind, but because EJ plays it with him, he has more fun and is more productive. It also reinforces the bond between them.

On the other hand, another person on EJ's team, Kathy, has the dominant talents of Includer and Developer in her CliftonStrengths results. [People exceptionally talented in the Includer theme accept others. They show awareness of those who are left out and make an effort to include them.] [People exceptionally talented in the Developer theme recognize and cultivate the potential in others. They spot the signs of each small improvement and derive satisfaction from evidence of progress.] EJ positions her as the "Welcoming Committee" to new team members, and she is also their *de facto* on-the-job trainer. Kathy loves the opportunity to bring new team members into the fold and make them feel comfortable, and the trainees benefit from a trainer who is patient, understanding, and who sees their potential.

Because EJ took the time to get to know each person on his team intimately and assign work that fit their individual talents, they have a strong sense of commitment. Additionally, because EJ sets the tone within the team for appreciation, members collaborate frequently. EJ takes time at every team meeting to review each one of the thirty-four talent themes in the CliftonStrengths Assessment. This consistent repetition builds both breadth and depth of knowledge within the team. While this may sound time-consuming and redundant, it really isn't, and the results have proven to be worth the investment. Plus, teammates are curious about the talents of their coworkers. When a team member needs assistance, she seeks out a coworker based on his talents. This creates reciprocity and camaraderie within the team. In addition, when it comes to setting goals, EJ uses the ASK method. He involves everyone in the process, so they have an increased sense of ownership over their work. Then EJ offers constant feedback, coaching, and support as everyone works toward their goals. Based on the exceptional results his team achieves and the way the entire team models the company's Behavioral Expectations, EJ is influential throughout the credit union. Other managers seek him out for advice.

Another way EJ acts with benevolence is in his reaction to mistakes. He never loses his temper or panics. EJ has honed his Top 5 talent of Self-Assurance. [People exceptionally talented in the Self-Assurance theme feel confident in their ability to take risks and manage their own lives. They have an inner compass that gives them certainty in their decisions.] He is confident in his ability to resolve any problem, and this sense of calm permeates the team. EJ uses errors as learning opportunities. In practice, learning is his primary method of discipline. This approach enhances people's knowledge, ultimately limiting mistakes. It also makes everyone feel safe. **The level of safety usually equals the level of trust.** EJ realizes that doing good for his team makes a good leader.

THE IMPORTANCE OF TIME AND ATTENTION IN BUILDING TRUST

Data shows that if a person on our team is feeling ignored, she is 98 percent more likely to be a person who throws the gum wrapper on the floor (and is miserable and vocal about it).[10] For most people, there is no worse feeling than being ignored. We demonstrate our care for people when we give them our time and attention in a customized way. If a person, for example, is reserved and private, we may recognize that how she likes attention is different than that of a person who craves social interaction. As we've pointed out, who we are is how we lead, which makes being able to modify our approach to each team member difficult. Couple that with everyone's unique preferences, and it gets very tricky. We can succeed by asking good questions, observing how each employee does things, and leveraging our deep knowledge of their CliftonStrengths Profile. Here are a few questions that can be meaningful conversation starters, which will help you provide personalized attention to each employee.

If you want thoughtful answers, give people time to think about their responses; if you want a person's reaction, ask a question spontaneously. I'd suggest sending these in advance of asking them to give each person time to think through their answers.

- What does your perfect day at work look like?
- What does a trusting relationship at work look like for you?
- What do I do that brings out the best in you?

10   The Gallup Business Journal: The No-Managers Organizational Approach Doesn't Work, 2016.

- What are the most important elements of a great workplace for you?
- What are your key needs at work that must be met for you to be your happiest?
- How can I be the best manager for you?
- While we will always have our monthly 1:1 meetings, how frequently do you think we should meet?
- What are the "manager don'ts" that I need to be aware of so I don't stifle you?

These aren't questions managers typically ask, so people might not have useful answers immediately. If that's the case, don't become discouraged. Keep observing, studying each person's dominant talent themes, and asking good questions. Adapt as you learn. Model this behavior, and others will follow suit. Eventually, you'll create an environment based on trust and care, and your team will willingly give their discretionary effort and live the Behavioral Expectations. And there won't be any gum wrappers on the floor.

As you read this, you might be thinking, "You're nuts, this is way too much time to spend. I'm already struggling to keep my head above water." I feel your pain, so I won't try another pep talk here about the obligation of your role and the impact you can have on another human being. Instead, I'll offer this antidote: do all of this in small bits of time each day as you work with your team. Take five minutes every day to study each person's CliftonStrengths results and bring what you've learned into general conversation. Most people enjoy talking about their strengths. You likely already observe your team members in action so just add the lens of talent themes. You can ask the many questions we've provided, a few at a time in your monthly meetings or your team meetings.

Take the approach that a jug fills more efficiently drop by drop rather than using a fire hose. As a personal example, I like to do card tricks when I'm working with teams. It breaks the ice, puts people at ease, and we get to have a little fun. While I'm far from an accomplished card magician, the tricks I perform aren't elementary and some take hours of practice to perform properly. I don't have hours to spend every day, so I allot fifteen minutes in my schedule every day to practice. Fifteen minutes every day is over an hour a week and about ninety-one hours a year. When I add in the open-space time from delayed start time of meetings, rescheduled calls or project deadlines being pushed back, my yearly total doubles. I build my proficiency gradually, but I build it all the same. You can do this, too. Allot fifteen minutes a day specifically to becoming more skilled at leading your team, and when spare time presents itself, use it wisely. **Don't waste any found time—develop your skills in the open spaces of your day.**

What we've explained will inevitably build trust. You

can't force trust. Force is the enemy in a situation like this. You have to let it evolve naturally, but you have to be the catalyst. **In my experience, a law of human dynamics that's close to universal is: you get what you give.** As people recognize that you're serving their desires, they'll respond in kind. If you enter every interaction considering the other person's perspective, I promise you the majority of people will reciprocate. If you're acting with benevolence, so, too, will your team members and most everyone else you come into contact with. It might take time for this to gel, especially if you have a challenging history with someone. If you persist over time, though, you will create the change you seek.

Treat each member of your team as an individual using the information you've just read, and they will feel cared for. They'll feel safe and empowered. They'll *want* to show up every day and perform at their best. Think of what you can accomplish when every member of your team is playing to their strengths and giving every ounce of discretionary effort. **You'll achieve the most sought-after state in the workplace: "Worvana." Nirvana at work!**

CASE STUDY: SURVEY SAYS...

In one company I worked for, there were over 10,000 employees. We set out to discover what made a great workplace, and we surveyed every employee in the company. In an effort to better understand what practices might separate average managers from high-performing managers, we asked one simple question: What does your manager do to make this a great place to work? When we studied the respondent data, there were two answers which were noted far more than any others: my manager accommodates my schedule, and my manager listens to me.

When we dug deeper into these two answers, what we found ties back to acting with benevolence and creating an environment blanketed with care. Employees at all levels appreciated flexibility in their schedules to work remotely when needed. This provided a work schedule that accommodated their lifestyle and allowed them to attend events, care for a sick child or elderly parent, and meet the repairman.

The positive feedback about managers listening went well beyond general conversation. These managers would ask team members for their advice about handling certain tasks where the employee had more knowledge. This display of vulnerability made the managers more approachable overall. These managers also solicited opinions on how to handle customer interactions, especially when the employee had an existing relationship with the customer the manager needed to talk with. These managers were the ones employees often sought out when they needed to vent. Additionally, they listened and eventually moved the conversation to devising solutions, but because they listened empathetically and without hurrying, employees felt heard and ready to fix the issue. Additionally, these managers sought feedback on how they were doing leading the team, and adjusted their approach based on comments employees gave. Employees reporting to these managers were more engaged than employees on other teams. **This research further illustrates the benefit of building caring relationships and trusting adults to do the right thing while offering them opportunities to live full lives.**

BENEVOLENCE CAN BE TRICKY

Positioning our team members to thrive using their talents oozes with benevolence. Here is an interesting example because of the circumstances: a team member with the Intellection talent theme in her Top 5 craved quiet time, but she worked in a call center. [People exceptionally talented in the Intellection theme are characterized by their intellectual activity. They are introspective and appreciate intellectual discussions.] If you manage a call center, how can you meet the need this person has to be alone on occasion in an environment that can be fairly frenetic and lacking solitude? The thought may be coming to you that the job is a bad fit for this employee, but it wasn't.

She also had other dominant talents, like Empathy and Restorative. [People exceptionally talented in the Empathy theme can sense other people's feelings by imagining themselves in others' lives or situations.] [People exceptionally talented in the Restorative theme are adept at dealing with problems. They are good at figuring out what is wrong and resolving it.] This made her one of the most effective employees at the call center because she excelled at calming down upset callers. She was able to put herself in their shoes and solve their problems with patience and determination. **None of us is just one talent theme; we are an amalgamation of our dominant talents.** As leaders, we need to recognize that it's rare when an employee perfectly fits a job. That's where leadership gets interesting. We need to modify the job to best fit the employee to increase engagement, which is what the call center manager did. He recognized the need for his team member to have a period away from the relentless pace the call center offered, so he routinely took her off call duty for one hour and gave her his office. He asked her to study the call centers' procedures to see what might be improved. The manager recognized this member of his team had a unique way of looking at things based on her Intellection talent theme, and he wanted her to use that talent to provide unthought-of ways to adjust their procedures. She got much needed quiet time while productively helping the team. **Improving lives comes from creating the best match between people's talents and the work that must be done.**

BENEVOLENCE REQUIRES COMMUNICATION

Every company I work with talks about improving their communication. As we start to dig a little deeper about what needs to be improved, there are four categories that seem to cover all the communication issues. I use the acronym FIST as a way to remember guidelines to fight off poor communication and to keep trust high.

- **Frequency.** How frequently do we communicate with people on our team? Do we keep them consistently in the loop? Do we meet regularly? Just like Behavioral Expectations that are lived, frequent communication lends a level of predictability to human interaction that can be comforting, as team members feel confident they will be kept informed of important happenings. I don't know many gum wrapper picking up employees who don't like to know what's going on in their company. If you're not sure if you should tell your team something, err on the side of overinforming. One company I worked with had gotten away from their standard meeting schedule because major initiatives consumed their time. The regularly scheduled quarterly all-staff meetings, weekly team meetings, and monthly one-on-one meetings stopped to ensure these major initiatives were completed on time. After months of missed meetings, the leadership team realized the negative impact. There was a real sense of people being disconnected from one another. There was a higher frequency of mixed messages, and the rumor mill picked up. This uncertainty increased fear and reduced trust. Discussions about the company's future got lost in the day to day. When the CEO realized she needed to return to the meeting schedule she had once diligently followed, these issues all gradually stopped as members of the team knew what was going on.

- **Involvement**. Do we seek feedback from our team and others in our company? Do we offer our ideas and solicit theirs? Our team will be more committed to an idea they participated in than one that's imposed upon them. Resist the urge to prioritize efficiency over effectiveness or dictate every action. Involve your team early and often. Once, there was a very confident CEO, who was a quick thinker with years of experience. He was also very affable. It was interesting to observe him interact with his Executive Team because he was magnificent at persuading everyone to follow his way of thinking. He would joke with people, listen to their thoughts, and then seamlessly the final decision inevitably ended up the way he wanted it to be. As time went on, members of the team became frustrated with his manipulative approach. They began to rebel, and the team became divided. The CEO's ego wouldn't let him involve others in important decisions. The less involved those leaders became, the less committed they became. **This formula is** accurate and predictive at any level of a company: **More Involvement = More Commitment, just as Less Involvement = Less Commitment.** The bigger problem for the company was when these Executive leaders started to ignore the gum wrappers, their team members began to do the same thing. Morale tanked, and productivity suffered. It was sad for a company that had a bright future.

• **Safety**. Do we make it safe for people to communicate with us? If people are fearful, they will be less open. That's not news. Most employees become reticent when they fear that their day will be made miserable if they speak up or if their job itself will be in jeopardy. As leaders, we must encourage everyone to voice their thoughts. Open conversations are in short supply at work. **Most employees think of things they never say.** That can reduce commitment and performance. The way to safety is to make sure every person we interact with feels she can say what she is thinking without fear of retaliation. I was talking to the Training Director at one credit union in particular who described an Executive Leader as "a man of the people." She talked about how anyone in the credit union could approach him about any issue—and it wasn't because he had a sympathetic ear. They talked to him because he would listen, ask questions, and help them come to a good decision. He'd offer his opinion if asked or if he felt he needed to. He was calm, caring, detailed, and reassuring. These characteristics made him approachable. Here is the interesting result. I facilitated a workshop with his direct reports and their peers. By comparison, his direct reports were the most well-informed about company happenings and the most willing to participate.

- **Transparency. There's an adage which advises, "Tell it first. Tell it all. Tell it yourself."** That defines transparency, and nothing like it builds trust. Make it a habit to share everything. Obviously, there will be some confidential items that we are prohibited from sharing, but aside from that there is little we shouldn't share. **Secrets breed distrust.** There was an organization I worked with where the CEO shared everything about the company; he truly held nothing back. Anyone could ask the CEO any question, and he would answer honestly. All information was shared, including discussions at the Board level. If someone asked something that needed to remain confidential, he explained why he couldn't answer it. The trust level in the company was high. The number of employees who picked up gum wrappers was unmatched, in part, because of the transparency. **Transparency answers one essential question: Do people in our company feel like insiders?** Making someone feel like an insider signifies a greater level of trust than being merely an employee. It also gives those insiders another reason to have faith in us as leaders. Related to the topic of transparency, according to Gallup's State of the American Workplace survey only 13 percent of employees strongly agree that their organization's leadership communicates effectively.[11] **Faith can move mountains, and doubt can create them.**

ACTIONABLE TOOLS FOR YOUR ORGANIZATION

Leading with benevolence is key to inspiring a team of employees who pick up the gum wrappers. Let's examine two tools you can use to help you do good.

TEAMWORK ANALYSIS

The Teamwork Analysis is a series of questions you can ask your team members. Use your judgment to decide if you should ask these questions at 1:1 meetings prior to having each team member share their answers at a team meeting. Ultimately, you will want everyone to share their answers with the rest of the team to build community and increase performance.

To start, provide everyone with a copy of the Teamwork Analysis in advance of the meeting so they have time

---

11   Gallup. "State of the American Workplace." Gallup.com. Accessed April 16, 2019. https://news. gallup.com/reports/178514/state-american-workplace.aspx.

to provide thoughtful answers. (A full copy is found in the Appendix.)

MY GREATEST CONTRIBUTION TO THE TEAM IS:	THREE THINGS THAT WOULD MAKE MY WORK LIFE EASIER ARE:
MY UNTAPPED POTENTIAL IS:	MY BIGGEST WORRY IS:

At the team meeting, I'd suggest using one question per meeting so you can spend some time deciding how to use the answers. Here are debriefing questions for each item that you can use if you need them. You'll notice that the second question refers to other teams. Your team can lead the way in supporting others in the company in meaningful ways. Don't miss the opportunity to be a difference-maker in your company. That said, if it feels overwhelming to think about other teams, stay focused on your team for now.

GREATEST CONTRIBUTION

* How can we best leverage one another's contributions?
* Can we show our appreciation to other teams for their meaningful contributions?

MAKE MY LIFE EASIER

* How can we lessen each other's burden?
* As a team, how can we make the life of other teams easier?

UNTAPPED POTENTIAL

* How can we tap into each other's potential?
* Whose potential in the company do we see being underutilized? Is there anything we can do to help that person realize his potential?

BIGGEST WORRY

* How can we minimize your worry?
* What are others in the company worrying about? Is there anything we can do to alleviate their stress?

Here are a few additional thoughts on carrying out this activity:

- As the leader, you should participate in (but not dominate) the conversation. Share your answers. Go last on the Greatest Contribution question and Make My Life Easier items but go first on the Biggest Struggle and the Biggest Worry for the quarter. This shows a sense of humility, an important quality in Acting with Benevolence.
- I'd take one item per meeting, giving it some time and effort.
- Come away with action plans. The worst thing you can do is talk about these items and never follow through.
- Check in during subsequent meetings to determine the benefit of the action plans.

RATE ME

I was explaining this activity to a leader who once told me what an idiotic idea it was to have his team evaluate him as a leader. "Why would I want someone to bash me?" he asked. To me, that seemed like a sad commentary on his view of leadership, which was obviously more aligned with an, "I'm the boss, and you'll do what I say" mentality. **Control is an illusion.** Remember one of the key questions of leadership: Do people get better in some way because they work for me? That question can help us surrender control and focus our effort on helping each of our team members become their best selves. People have minds of their own. That's what makes leading so difficult. Remember those astronomical odds of finding someone with your same Top 5 in the CliftonStrengths Assessment? Because everyone on our team is different and because people can be at different points in their learning curve on various tasks, it helps to get feedback on our performance to be sure we're leading effectively.

This is a straightforward activity, a full copy of which is found in the Appendix for easy access. Here's how it works:

In advance of monthly one-on-one meetings with team members, make sure each person comes prepared with specific answers to these questions:

- On a scale of one to five, with five being high, how would you rate me as your manager?
- If the rating is a five, ask, "What am I doing that makes you rate me that way?"
- If the rating is anything other than a five, ask, "What can I do to make it a five?"
- If you're uncomfortable asking this set of questions, here is an alternative question that's effective: What is one thing I can do to be a better leader for you?

Here are a few thoughts on carrying out this activity:

- This set of questions will put the level of trust between you and each team member to the test. If people feel safe, they'll be honest; if not, they won't.
- After you've spoken to each team member, evaluate if everyone opened up or if only some did. This can be an indication that your relationships are uneven through the team.
- As people provide answers, avoid becoming defensive or explaining away what they are saying. Instead, listen to understand and ask clarifying questions. If you do this, your level of trust will be bolstered.
- For each person, develop a plan of action. That means settling on specific behaviors people want from you. For those who gave you a five, ask them to provide you with specific behaviors so you can continue to repeat those.
- Follow through on the action plan and check in to see how it is going.
- Ask this set of questions at least twice a year.

Acting with benevolence is critical to building trust and pushing everyone to be the best person they can be. You're establishing the underpinnings of the relationship that you will call on in good times and bad.

Leadership, in a word, is about influence. Our next element of great leadership, Celebrate the Individual, will add to your influence.

CHAPTER 8

CELEBRATE THE INDIVIDUAL

No one ever left a job for feeling over appreciated. You've probably never heard a coworker complain, "I have to find a new job. My manager just praises me too much." I'll bet you've heard the opposite, though. Meaningful recognition is a key element in creating engaged employees who pick up the gum wrapper.

Jesse, a District Manager, asks each of his team members a very important question: "When you do outstanding work, who do you want to know about it, both inside the company and out?" Every person has their clan—people they are close to—whether that's family members, friends, or colleagues. The question Jesse asked is one each of us should ask members of our team. Sometimes the response can lead to unforgettable moments.

When Jesse asked this question of David, one of his branch managers, his response caught Jesse off guard. David wanted his two-year-old daughter to know he'd done outstanding work. Jesse didn't flinch, tucked away the information, and finished his monthly one-on-one. On his way out of the branch, Jesse asked a coworker to call him when David's wife and daughter came by the office. David lived in the same neighborhood as the branch, and his wife would occasionally stop by for lunch.

About two weeks later, David's wife came into the office with their daughter to see David. The coworker who Jesse spoke with on his way out of the branch quickly called and alerted him. Jesse happened to be about ten minutes away and told the coworker to stall David's wife and daughter until he arrived. When Jesse got to the branch, he said hello to the employees and then walked into David's office. Jesse greeted David's wife, exchanged pleasantries with David, and then got down on one knee and said to David's daughter, "Your daddy is one of the best employees that we have at our company. We're lucky to have him." Tears streamed down David's face.

Consider that piece of recognition versus the standard "atta boy." It would have been easier for Jesse to never ask who should know about David's successes and just tell David what a good job he was doing. After all, that's the conventional approach. Think, though, about the difference in impact: no contest. **That's what it means to Celebrate the Individual: being intentional about building a level of intimacy in the relationship and taking subsequent actions that make each person who reports to us feel not only appreciated but celebrated.**

There's a footnote to David's story. Soon after that memorable day, a member of David's family got sick, and David had to resign. David and his family moved a few hours away to help care for their relative. While Jesse was in the process of finding a replacement for David's position, the branch was short-staffed. Saturdays were especially difficult on the remaining employees. After getting permission from his new employer, David told Jesse that he'd come back to town and work Saturdays until the vacancy his departure created was filled.

When was the last time you heard of someone driving four hours and giving up Saturdays to help out a former employer? I'll grant you, that's an extreme example, but it speaks to the power of a relationship built on mutual admiration and high regard.

Nancy, a CIO, once asked this same question of one of her project managers. Vincent indicated that he'd like his wife to know when he performed well. After Vincent finished a complicated project on time and under budget, Nancy recognized him in a team meeting. Vincent was appreciative of the accolades and the good-natured ribbing from his colleagues. With that project in the rearview mirror, Vincent moved on to the next one without much thought about the question Nancy had asked him a few months earlier.

A few days later, Vincent got home from work and his wife showed him a card that was sent to her by Nancy. Nancy wrote how appreciative she was of Vincent's work and what an asset he was to the company. There was also a gift card to their favorite restaurant.

While these examples of recognition are uncommon in most workplaces, they don't take a tremendous amount of extra time or money. Sometimes, it's just a matter of realizing their importance. The payoff in loyalty created by these gestures is incredible because they show a true sense of knowing what is important to each person and caring enough to follow through.

When we recognize people in what they consider a meaningless way, our thoughtfulness can be misinterpreted. Susan, for example, was a twenty-something young woman who worked at the front desk of a five-star hotel. She was an exemplary performer, serving customers and taking care of problems all day long, always with a smile and composure. Susan regularly went above and beyond her job duties, too: when new team members joined her at the front desk, Susan consistently took it upon herself to train them. This minimized the struggles of her inexperienced coworkers who were learning the reservation system while trying to serve guests. Susan enjoyed seeing people grow and improve. She remembered feeling underwhelmed at her own training—so much so that she felt inept and unprepared for many of her initial shifts. Susan didn't want anyone else to feel that way, so she took it upon herself to see that they didn't. She also had great pride in her organization and wanted the hotel to run smoothly and succeed. She always picked up the gum wrappers.

Susan's manager, Casey, recognized her work and wanted to do something special for her. Casey loved to get massages, manicures, and pedicures. Thinking that would be a nice surprise, she jumped through hoops with the corporate office to get a $100 gift card for Susan to use at the hotel spa. On delivery day, Casey excitedly walked up and handed the gift card to Susan, explaining her gratitude for Susan shouldering extra responsibility and going the extra mile for guests. Susan thanked her but the conversation quickly went dead. Casey had expected Susan to gush with enthusiasm, not be indifferent. Casey didn't understand where things had gone wrong, and she resented Susan for not being more grateful of her efforts to secure the gift card. Casey later learned that Susan didn't like massages. A spa service that sounded lovely to Casey sounded horrible to Susan. Instead of the gift card telling Susan, "You're a superb member of the team and I appreciate you," it said, "I don't really care enough to know what's important to you. But I know what I like, so I'll just give you that."

AT THE HEART OF CELEBRATING

When it comes to meaningful recognition, the Clifton-Strengths Assessment can be an invaluable tool. For example, if a member of your team has the talent theme of Responsibility in her Top 5, giving her added authority may be a sure sign that you've recognized her knack for impeccable follow-through and want to reward that. [People exceptionally talented in the Responsibility theme take psychological ownership of what they say they will do. They are committed to stable values such as honesty and loyalty.] If someone on the team has the talent theme of Strategic and you assign him a complex problem, he may thrive on the challenge. [People exceptionally talented in the Strategic theme create alternative ways to proceed. Faced with any given scenario, they can quickly spot the relevant patterns and issues.] These are subtle rewards you can offer that celebrate each person's individuality by playing to their well-honed talents.

Putting the Strengths-Based Philosophy of developing, sharpening and honoring everyone's Strengths causes celebration at two levels. First, since our greatest opportunity for exponential growth comes from our areas of Strength, all of us will become better at those things at which we already excel. We can celebrate amazing accomplishments. Second, by giving each person what she wants more of based on her Strengths we can celebrate who she is in a way that's significant to her. This way of working, because it is personalized and positive, creates a dynamic wave in the team that everyone can ride to higher ground. The job becomes easier, the stress and pressure are reduced and the relationships, unencumbered, are free to grow.

BEING THE OFFICE HERO IS OVERRATED

A fallacy of leading others is that we must know all the answers and solve all the problems. That's an unrealistically high bar to reach. I do believe that everything rises and falls with leadership, but that doesn't mean we as leaders must be all and do all; it does mean we have to know our team members intimately and use their abilities effectively. Successful leaders are the ones who understand that they are part of a team, focus on using their best and help others be their best.

You'll find your employees are better than you at certain things and that you're better than them at certain things. That's how a team is usually organized. After all, if you go to see the Rolling Stones (a band is a team), you don't want Mick Jagger playing the drums. You want him singing and dancing. Share the responsibilities according to talent.

I worked with one leader who admittedly was not good with numbers, yet he was responsible for his department's budget. There was someone on his team who had the Analytical talent theme in her Top 5 and was gifted with numbers. [People exceptionally talented in the Analytical theme search for reasons and causes. They have the ability to think about all the factors that might affect a situation.] During budget season, the manager and this team member met to discuss the budget and review the template provided by the Accounting Department. Then the team member completed the budget and, met routinely with the manager to scrutinize each month's results. When variances or concerns arose, the employee and the manager worked through them.

In this case, the employee loved the extra responsibility. She got to do something she enjoyed and was good at, allowing her to make an important contribution to the team. She also got to develop new skills based on a once underutilized talent. The manager was freed up to do things he was better at and enjoyed more. **One person playing to her strength and another avoiding his weakness—a formula for team success uncon-**

strained by formal authority and job descriptions.
Many managers, feeling the need to work on an important task like the budget, would be reluctant to surrender control knowing full well the work will be draining and time consuming. When someone on the team is better at something than we are, surrender the need for control and the notion that people are defined by their stated job duties. Performance and solidarity will soar.

CELEBRATE DEVELOPMENT

Another way to celebrate people is to develop them. Invest in people to help them become better today than they were yesterday. Development can come in many forms. New tasks, special projects, committees, training, and coaching are the major ones. Development isn't necessarily about promotional opportunities. It's also about helping people improve in their current job. The more breadth and depth a person has in her current role, the more confident she will feel and the more she can contribute.

Another way to apply the ASK Model (ASK stands for Agreed-Upon, Strengths-Based and Known) of goal setting which we outlined in the practice of *Manage to Outcomes* is to mutually devise stretch assignments that focus on development. Once the assignment is in place, take time to observe your team member in action and then debrief by asking a series of questions that might include:

- What do you think you did well?
- What could you have done better?
- What would you do differently next time?
- What did you learn that you can apply going forward?

These four questions are just the beginning. Probe based on the answers. Tie talents to how the work was done and point out nuances that may have been missed. Lead your team member to places he might not have gotten on his own. Draw the learning out of him. Always encourage and instill confidence.

When it comes to development, don't forget about long-tenured employees. Many times, these people, especially if they perform well, are put on managerial autopilot to keep plowing through the work. **Don't confuse experience with not having a need to develop.** Everyone is different, but no matter the level of experience, development opportunities are usually invigorating and signal an investment in a person. Do this with everyone who reports to you, and you can be proud of the positive impact you're having. You'll eliminate the dropped gum wrappers.

ACTIONABLE TOOLS FOR YOUR ORGANIZATION

The more questions you ask, the more you will learn about people. Here are additional questions you can use to start meaningful discussions to ensure you are recognizing and developing people on your team—a full copy of which is also included in the Appendix for easy access. These dovetail with the 1:1 Coaching Guide questions also found in the Appendix. Use one or two of these questions in your monthly one-on-one dialogues. Probe and prod the answers to get clarity and, of critical importance, follow through.

RECOGNITION QUESTIONS:

- If you were me, how would you best recognize you?
- What kind of work do you deem recognition worthy?
- What was the worst piece of recognition you ever received? What made it the worst?
- Who was the manager, teacher, or coach who gave you the recognition you enjoyed the most? What did s/he do?
- What kind of recognition makes you feel the best?
- What motivates you?
- What do you find inspirational about your work?
- If you were isolated on an island, besides people, what would you make sure you had with you that you couldn't live without?

DEVELOPMENT QUESTIONS:

- Who are the mentors in your life?
- What did you learn from your mentors?
- How can I help you improve?
- What's your dream job look like? What do you need to get there?
- If money didn't matter, what would you do with your time?
- What do you want to master so you feel most proficient in your job?
- What one wish do you have for your development?

CHAPTER 9

WORKING FOR THE GREATER GOOD

Create the company you want to work for by build-ing bridges with your peers. That's really at the heart of working for the greater good. **The pressure to hit our goals can make us selfish.** It makes sense. After all, we work in large part to fund the things we want in life. The more successful we are, the more we can enjoy. The insid-ious pressure can create unintended consequences.

Here's an example: the banking industry tends to have high teller turnover. Mindful of his budget, the COO of a small bank opted to have the tellers' business cards printed with a blank line rather than names so the bank wouldn't incur the costs to reprint business cards in the event someone left the organization. Each time a teller handed a business card to a customer, he'd need to pause and write his name on the line. The COO was saving the company money and trying to ensure he hit his budget. The tellers, however, saw their blank business cards as a demoralizing sign that they weren't important or long for the bank. Well-intentioned people can take actions that make sense for *their* goals but not think about the impact on others. Shortly after the nameless business cards were introduced, they were shelved, and proper business cards were issued to all tellers. If the COO had collaborated with the Chief Retail Officer on the front end of this decision, the negative impact on the tellers would have been averted.

This example is a common occurrence of how leaders look out for their own function without regard for their colleagues. It's rarely malicious; it's just the default thinking brought on by pressure. As a leader working for the greater good, it's our job to be a catalyst for bridging these gaps and bringing the organization together. You might be thinking, "Why should I bother with this? My goals are my primary responsibility, and others have their own goals they are working toward. If we all work toward our goals, success will follow. Even if they don't hit their goals but I hit mine, that's still good by me." The danger of thinking this way is that it leads to teams and individuals to work only for themselves. In truth, we need the support of others to hit our goals. **Organizations are interdependent entities with functions relying on one another to succeed.**

SUPPORT IS INVALUABLE

In one organization, tension ran high between the Sales Team and the Accounting Team. Accounting was upset with Sales because they didn't complete their expense reports for their company credit cards properly or timely. Sales was commission-based and didn't want to waste time filling out onerous reports they saw stealing valuable selling time. The battle lines were drawn. Each complained about the other to anyone who would listen.

One day, the Sales Manager approached the Accounting Manager to ask how they might be able to resolve the problem. The Accounting Manager's initial reply was, "Just fill out the damn reports correctly and submit them when they're due." The Sales Manager expected that and didn't get defensive. Her response focused, instead, on trying to make the process better so her team would complete the reports properly and timely. The Sales Manager asked what the essential elements of the report were so perhaps they could be slimmed down, making the Sales Team's job easier and still provide Accounting the information they needed.

The Accounting Manager didn't warm to the idea because it meant changing the format they'd used for years. As they talked about the virtue of a new report, the Accounting Manager began to see the benefits not only to his team but to others in the company. The essential-only data would simplify settlements for his team, and it would likely make completion of the reports easier on the rest of the company. The Accounting Manager and Sales Manager began to craft a new report together. Once they finished, the Accounting Manager shared the report with his team to get their input. They, too, saw the benefit of this leaner report.

One member of the team made a few adjustments, which the Sales Manager agreed made sense when the Accounting Manager showed her the revised version. The Sales Manager showed the condensed report to her team, and they loved it. Together, the two teams piloted the report. It worked well, with both sides making minor edits. The final version was shared at a Senior Leadership Team Meeting and was met with enthusiasm. The Sales Manager pointed out that this saved her team on average four hours a month, or more than another full week annually to make calls and drive business. The Accounting Manager noted that the new report also saved his team time that would be used to streamline other processes. The CEO was the most enthusiastic of all. Not about the new report, but the way the two leaders collaborated and upheld the company's Behavioral Expectations.

This kind of support sets up a culture that signals, "I am my colleague's keeper." When people work for the greater good, politics, manipulation, and self-serving motives are decreased, and everyone is free to do their jobs with less concern. **You want to build a company where no one has to have your back, not because it isn't supportive but because no one's trying to stab you.**

Sadly, in most companies, politics and manipulation are a fact of daily life. Here's an example that's typical: a Sales Director and a member of his team disagreed about whether a product catalog should be sent to customers. Because the company offers over fifty products, the Sales Director thought customers wouldn't read a lengthy document. He was also concerned that it might even diminish the efforts of the sales team if customers quickly glanced at the catalog, missing many of the differentiating factors, before filing it away.

The employee, still unhappy with her manager's decision, went straight to her former manager, who had been promoted to the company President. The employee explained her reasons for wanting the catalog mailed and, instead of supporting the Sales Director or calling him to discuss his reasoning, the President sent the Sales Director an email detailing the reasons why the product catalog should be sent to their customer base. Needless to say, the Sales Director no longer trusts his employee or his boss. He now only communicates with his employee by email, so he has a record of everything that's been discussed. He's also stopped making many decisions, instead deferring them to his boss. To call him demoralized would be an understatement. Gum wrappers are all over his office floor.

A more subtle example occurs when a manager doesn't support another department but piles on about their error. Here's a common example: The Customer Service Department hired a new employee. The department manager sent a request to IT to ready a laptop for the new employee. IT delivered the laptop on time, but it didn't work properly. The manager called the IT department and notified them of the problem. IT worked on it remotely and even sent a technician to the manager's location to physically work on the laptop. The technician made a one-hour drive. Meanwhile, the Customer Service Department Manager complained to her manager, The Chief Revenue Officer, about the problem.

The Chief Revenue Officer, feeling like she had to support her manager, called the IT Director to complain. So, of course, the IT Director got more of his staff involved. All the while, the Customer Service Manager was badmouthing IT, ignoring the fact that IT was working feverishly to correct the problem remotely and with the on-site technician.

The other thing that's occurring in this scenario is that no real work is getting done. Productivity is halted while the battle discussion takes center stage. There is no argument that the laptop should have been delivered in proper working order, but all of the extra drama created by the Customer Service Manager was unnecessary. It left the new employee questioning his decision to join the company and created a rift between the departments that lingers. Gum wrappers litter the hallways between their departments.

Think what a difference it would have made if the Customer Service Manager gave the benefit of the doubt to the IT Team and explained to the new employee that IT just missed installing a piece of software, but they were overall excellent service partners to everyone in the company—which was true. Additionally, a call to IT explaining the issue and respectfully asking for a fix to the problem was all that was needed. There was no need to escalate the problem, especially when IT was responsive to the manager's initial request. The way problems are resolved among coworkers can strengthen support or erode it.

There's also the story of the department manager who rebelled against efforts made by the company to create unity through celebrating a growth milestone. The company regularly celebrated events and asked all locations to participate. This was a time of joy and reenergizing for employees, recognizing everyone's efforts in helping the company grow. In an email to the sponsor of the event, the department manager of one location claimed his team didn't have time to participate. The manager's email was curt and demeaning, noting what a waste of money and time the celebration was. This department manager's boss, not wanting to confront the situation, sat idly by offering zero support for the corporate initiative. The sponsor of the event was astonished by the responses of the department manager and his boss. Her attempts to persuade the two leaders to join in were ignored. In the end, theirs was the only location not to participate, and that fact spread like wildfire through the rest of the company creating a lingering feeling of bad blood. Gum wrappers abound.

In my experience, these last three examples are far more common than the first collaborative one, which is an unfortunate reason why cohesion in companies is so rare. Many managers set up a dynamic of "our team" versus everyone else, thinking it will unite their team. It might but at the expense of the entire organization. This tact isn't only unhealthy, it's destructive as it cracks the corporate armor by creating a slew of subcultures. Toxic competition within our walls becomes the norm. As leaders, if we want to create an *us against them* mentality, it should be our entire company rallying against our competition. There's plenty out there to target. Go back to that first example. Think about working at a company where everyone is collaborating like the Sales Manager and the Accounting Manager. It's a place where everyone is working together for the common good and the success of the business. That's a sought-after environment—one where people can lower their guard, raise their desire to help, and concentrate on doing good work. This kind of support makes it easy for every person to do their job in a relaxed and confident manner because they know there is an entire company of people to help with any problem. Most of us work better when we feel better. The better we feel, the fewer gum wrappers litter our offices.

WHAT DOES GOOD COLLABORATION LOOK LIKE?

I once worked with a highly collaborative leader, Sofia. In our team meetings, she would set aside time on the agenda to have discussions about how other teams were doing. She would have coffee with people in different departments or connect with them in person or by phone, always asking, "How can we best support you?" Sofia would collect that data and present it at our meetings for discussion, and together we'd discuss how we could support the other team. Sofia had the spirit of collaboration and unity, everyone thought well of her, and she had a tremendous amount of influence. Not surprisingly, support was reciprocal. When we needed help from another department, we got it immediately and without question. At the end of the day, our company's execution significantly improved because of the strong relationships Sofia helped to forge among departments.

Because the root of collaboration is working in the best interest of another, it's also an act of building trust—a key to organizational success. An environment without trust is cautious and protective; if you put your team members in such an environment, it will be hard for them to perform effectively and enjoy their work. It's much like putting a healthy fish in a contaminated tank; you *know* the fish will die. Instead, create good habits around collaboration: support other departments, don't battle, work as a team throughout the entire organization, and prioritize organizational cohesion over individual gains. A few reasonable action steps can include redirecting team member complaints about other departments, standing up for other departments, asking members of your team to volunteer on cross-functional projects, setting up lunches with other departments, and getting feedback from those departments your team works with most closely to learn if there is anything you can do to work more effectively together.

The time to build collaboration is not when everything is crumbling around you. As President John F. Kennedy said, "The time to repair the roof is when the sun is shining." **Build your relationships *before* you need them.** That way, when a problem does occur, the parties will already know one another well enough to be open to hearing a different perspective.

BEHAVIORAL EXPECTATIONS AND STRENGTHS LEAD TO THE GREATER GOOD

Well-established Behavioral Expectations followed by everyone in the company generate consistency in how people treat one another. This is a great benefit when it comes to working across the company. We know how we'll work together because that's what we've agreed to. This level of predictability and built-in respect helps when it comes to collaboration because even though we might not work closely with someone all the time, we can still work with them in a way that is in concert with the Behavioral Expectations. This takes the guesswork out of how to interact with someone, which saves time and reduces stress. We have common bonds which can be the seeds of a trusting relationship.

If your organization has a repository for everyone's Strengths, you can review those before you meet with someone you don't work with frequently. That will offer you some clues on the person's preferences. For example, if you're about to start a project with the Marketing Department and know you'll be interfacing with a particular person many times over the next few weeks, you can look up her Strengths to gain insight into how to best work with her. Here's how that looks in action: say you're not a detailed person, but you grasp concepts quickly and well. When you look up the information for your contact in the Marketing Department, you see she has the talent theme of Input. [People exceptionally talented in the Input theme have a need to collect and archive. They may accumulate information, ideas, artifacts or even relationships.] You know you'll benefit from her genius of researching to find what is needed and her ability to locate in her files just about anything you discuss. Additionally, her curious nature may move the discussion in productive ways it may not have gone without her inquisitiveness. If she asks for time to search for information, you won't be caught off guard because you've made allowances for it. Instead, you'll be prepared to discuss a reasonable deadline that allows her the time she needs to feel good about the work she produces.

ACTIONABLE TOOLS FOR YOUR ORGANIZATION

Along with living and reinforcing the Behavioral Expectations and learning people's Strengths, here are three key actions you can take to be a unifier in your organization. These build on one another.

- First, measure your greater good mindset using the continuum found in the Appendix. Really think about what you've just read as you work through the questions associated with the continuum. Having this mindset shows everyone you come into contact with that you're a steward of the company. Your modeling may get others to follow suit which will benefit your organization.

- Next, broaden the team's understanding of the company's direction and your role in that. One way to achieve this is to invite your manager and other higher-level managers to your team meetings to further explain the direction of the company and why certain actions are occurring. Have the guest speakers explain how they see your team's work connected to the vision and mission of the company. With your team, prepare questions for your guest speaker that will provide meaningful information. Depending on the preference of the speaker you may want to send these questions in advance so she can provide thoughtful answers. Insightful questions include, "What is one thing our team can do to have the greatest impact on the success of the company?" and "What aren't we doing that we should start doing to make the company more successful?" Refer to the Appendix for a full list of potential questions. Remember, you want this to be a good experience for both the speaker and your team. It's a meeting meant to further the team's understanding of where you fit in and how you can contribute. The added benefit is that these meetings showcase your team to others in the organization. So many times, when a more senior leader joins a team meeting, it's crickets. No one talks. In addition, sometimes the conversation can get a bit uncomfortable if there is a lot of complaining. If you've been following the process outlined through the book, this shouldn't happen as your team is engaged and communicating empathically.

- Finally, take action by initiating support for other teams in the company. Use what you've learned from meetings with your manager or other higher-level managers. Follow Sofia's approach noted above. Meet with other teams and have them attend your meetings. Do what you can to lend a hand. Given your workload you might not be able to spend significant time, but any thing you can do will make a difference and cement your team's reputation as trusted partners. Other leaders will reciprocate when you need assistance.

This series of actions will cause your influence, and that of your team, to soar in the company. You will become a model for others to emulate. The greater good mindset reinforces the culture you're trying to build.

CONCLUSION

In a workplace that leverages the CliftonStrengths Assessment, lives Behavioral Expectations, and cultivates leaders who serve others, there are no gum wrappers on the floor. Discretionary effort is given freely. Employees don't dread Mondays. Work energizes teams, not drains them. The organization produces a better product with a team of fulfilled, enthusiastic, capable employees and leaders who serve as rocket fuel for growth.

PUTTING THE PROCESS INTO ACTION

If this process of transforming your organization's approach to people sounds like it will require a substantial amount of effort, that's because it will. It's the reality of building something magnificent. Besides, maintaining a poorly run organization takes great effort. It's just a different kind of effort—coping with the stress created by high turnover, correcting errors created by inexperienced or uncommitted employees, trying to retain customers who receive poor service, and more. Either way, we've got to put the work in. The only decision is whether to put it in to building a great company or to put it in to salvaging the company.

Starting isn't really the hard part, it's sustaining this that can be difficult. To start, consider these steps:

* Have everyone on your team take the CliftonStrengths Assessment. Then, use the activities I outlined earlier as well as the online resources Gallup has available. Go slowly with the activities, but remain consistent by keeping Strengths as an agenda item in team meetings and monthly one-on-one dialogues. If you can afford an expert, I'd recommend contacting a Gallup Certified Strengths Coach in your area. When dealing with something as consequential as the health of your workplace, qualified and knowledgeable coaches are worth the expense. Find one at gallupstrengthcenter. com.
* Once you've gained momentum with Strengths, develop Behavioral Expectations within the team. You can use the process I've outlined or some variation. Then, keep discussing these at team meetings and monthly one-on-one dialogues.
* Begin incorporating the Leadership Practices dis-

cussed in this book. Add them to your repertoire in a way that is comfortable for you. Again, go slowly but consistently.

WORDS OF ENCOURAGEMENT

Thank you for taking the time to read this book. Now is the time to put your knowledge into practice. You'll make a difference for everyone around you. Anybody can go to a job they don't love, be semi-unhappy, and then go home to do it all over again the next day. Unfortunately, that describes a majority of employees today. Work doesn't have to be this way. Wouldn't you like to be part of something special? What if work felt like an amazing place to express yourself and make a meaningful contribution? What if you could form strong relationships and do work you enjoyed *every day*?

You can. But remember, great vision requires great effort. Stay the course and try not to get discouraged. Sometimes, trying something new can be met with resistance. However, as your team sees the benefits of an organization transformed, that resistance will melt away.

The time to act is now. Don't wait for inspiration to strike. Look around at the faces in your company; isn't that inspiration enough to improve their lives and yours? Will you show up as that leader, the change agent for making the organization and its people better?

Create the kind of legacy where people think about your leadership long after they've left, where they're inspired to make their organization gum-wrapper free, too. **That's the best kind of leader to be—remembered for the difference you made in people's lives.**

APPENDIX

CLIFTONSTRENGTHS

TALENT NEEDS ACTIVITY

Step One: Circle your top five talent themes.

Step Two: Based on the rating scale found below, rate how frequently each need gets met at work.

Step Three: Work with your teammates to answer the follow-up questions listed in the questionnaire below.

Note: This activity and more context around it can be found in Chapter 3.

Achiever:	Freedom to get my work done on my own schedule
Activator:	Less discussion and more action
Adaptability:	Present pressure that demands an immediate response
Analytical:	Obtain the data I need
Arranger:	An environment with multiple and simultaneous tasks
Belief:	A cause or mission for my work
Command:	Challenges and conflicts
Communication:	A sounding board, an audience for conversation
Competition:	A yardstick for comparison
Connectedness:	To be part of something bigger than myself
Consistency:	Standard operating procedures
Context:	Relevant background for discussions and decisions

Deliberative:	Time to weigh the pros and cons before needing to decide
Developer:	Someone to invest in
Discipline:	A structured and organized environment
Empathy:	The freedom to express my emotions
Focus:	A goal to establish priorities
Futuristic:	Opportunities to talk and think about the future
Harmony:	Areas of agreement and common ground
Ideation:	Freedom to explore the possibilities without restraints
Includer:	Room for everyone
Individualization:	Individual expectations that are created to fit the person
Input:	Time to research and a place to store my things/information
Intellection:	Time for reflection and thought
Learner:	Exposure to new information
Maximizer:	Quality to be valued as much as quantity
Positivity:	An upbeat environment
Relator:	Time for one-on-one interactions
Responsibility:	Freedom to take ownership of my work

Restorative:	Problems that need to be solved
Self-Assurance:	Freedom to act independently
Significance:	An appreciative audience that brings out the best in me
Strategic:	Freedom to make mid-course corrections
WOO:	The need for social variability

QUESTIONNAIRE: TALENT NEEDS

- How frequently is each of your dominant talent's needs being met?

    5 = All of the time

    4 = Most of the time

    3 = Some of the time

    2 = Occasionally

    1 = Rarely, if at all

- What actions can you take to increase the frequency of your needs being met?

- How can you help others on the team meet their needs?

EDGE ACTIVITY

Step One: List your top five strengths.

Step Two: Review the list of EDGE words and phrases, and underline those that resonate with you.

Step Three: Answer the questions in the questionnaire.

Note: This activity and more context around it can be found in Chapter 3.

Achiever: Tireless, strong work ethic, leads by example, go-getter, hungry

Activator: Self-starter, fire-starter, energy sources, fearless

Adaptability: Flexible, comfortable in times of change, easy to get along with, go with the flow

Analytical: Well thought out, logical, deep, thorough, comfortable with numbers, figures, and charts

Arranger: Flexible, organizer, juggler, aligning and realigning tasks to find the most productive configuration possible, efficient, conductor

Belief: Passionate, steadfast, know where I stand, altruistic, family-oriented, ethical, responsible

Command: Charisma, direct, driven, inspirational, easy to follow, clear, concise

Communication: Storyteller, great presence, easy to talk to, energizer, entertaining, charismatic

Competition: Driven, motivated, number one, measurement-oriented, winner

Connectedness: Spiritual, "doesn't sweat the small stuff," strong faith, always looking at the big picture, helps others see purpose, unifier

Consistency: Just, repeatability, policy maker, rule follower

Context: Has a robust historical frame of reference, learns lessons from the past, knows how things came to be, can leverage knowledge of the past

Deliberative: Good judgment, identifies risk, makes solid decisions, can plan for the unexpected

Developer: Grows talent in others, teacher, coach, enjoys helping others succeed, invests in others

Discipline: High productivity and accuracy because of the ability to structure, breaks down complex into steps, great planners, promotes efficiency

Empathy: Creates trust, brings healing, knows just what to say/do, customizes approach to others' emotions

Focus: Point person, disciplined, purposeful, laser-like precision, identifies important areas quickly, goal setter and goal getter

Futuristic:	Imaginative, creative, visionary, even prophetic, inspiring
Harmony:	Negotiator, can see both sides of a situation, great at asking questions, able to arrive at consensus, great facilitator
Ideation:	Improves on the existing, agile mind, creates novel approaches, can deliver ideas in bunches
Includer:	Invites others in, caring, engages others, sensitive, takes up for others
Individualization:	Sees the uniqueness in all individuals, intuitively knows that "one size doesn't fit all," appreciates the differences in others
Input:	Great resource, knowledgeable, excellent memory, mind for detail, collects interesting things, excellent conversationalist
Intellection:	Excellent thinker, enjoys musing, capable of deep and philosophical thought, able to work alone, offers an unthought-of perspective
Learner:	Always learning, catches on quickly, interested in many things, finds life intriguing, rarely makes the same mistake twice
Maximizer:	Mastery, success, excellence, working within the best, dissatisfied with good enough

Positivity: Enthusiastic, lighthearted, energetic, generous with praise, optimistic, grateful

Relator: Caring, trusting, a great friend, generous

Responsibility: Committed, accountable, independent, trusted, conscientious, reliable

Restorative: Problem solver, troubleshooter, finds improvements and solutions, courageous in difficult situations

Self-Assurance: Self-confident, strong inner compass, risk-taker, makes independent decisions

Significance: Seeks outstanding performance, does things of importance, independent, swagger

Strategic: Anticipates alternatives, intuitive, sees different paths, picks up on clues quickly

WOO: Outgoing, people-oriented, networked, rapport-building

QUESTIONNAIRE: EDGE ACTIVITY

• What do I bring to the team?

• Based on the power your talents give you, what actions can you take to best leverage your gifts to enhance your contribution to the team?

• What actions will you take now?

OVERUSE ACTIVITY

Step One: List your top five strengths.

Step Two: Review the list of words and underline those that you do.

Step Three: Pick one word from each talent theme that you underlined to stop doing.

Step Four: Answer the questions in the questionnaire.

Note: This activity and more context around it can be found in Chapter 3.

Achiever: Unbalanced, overcommitted, can't say no, burning the candle at both ends, too concentrated on work

Activator: Ready-fire-aim, loose cannon, speak before you think, in left field (because others haven't caught up)

Adaptability: Directionless, indecisive, sheepish, inconclusive, whimsical

Analytical: Rude, short, tough, never satisfied with the answer, too many questions

Arranger: Lack of structure, too flexible, don't follow the existing rules or procedures, constantly changing priorities, lack of consistent vision

Belief: Stubborn, set in their ways, elitist, unaccepting of other ideas, opinionated, goody-two-shoes

Command:	Bossy, domineering, rude, abrupt, short, strong-willed, inflexible, stubborn
Communication:	Blabbermouth, poor listener, self-absorbed, show-off, always needs attention
Competition:	Sore loser, not a team player, puts down others, self-centered, confrontational
Connectedness:	Passive, naïve, too idealistic, wishy-washy
Consistency:	"By the book," inflexible, unwilling to customize/individualize
Context:	Slow to move and react to change, closed-minded, lives in the past
Deliberative:	Standoffish, aloof, cautious, slow to take action, afraid to act
Developer:	Not an individual contributor, wastes time on low-potential people, spectator
Discipline:	Overbearing, rigid, mechanized, can't handle change
Empathy:	"Soft," moody, over-involved
Focus:	Absorbed, tough to relax, intense, stressed
Futuristic:	Dreamer, "Fantasy Island," out in left field, lacks pragmatism
Harmony:	Weak, indecisive, non-confrontational, avoids conflict

Ideation: Serendipitous, lacks follow-through, creates more work

Includer: Indiscriminate, unable to decide, generous to a fault

Individualization: Unable to synthesize when it comes to people, has difficulty placing group above individual, difficulty making people decisions

Input: Knows a lot of worthless information, packrat, cluttered house-cluttered mind, boring conversationalist

Intellection: A loner, slow to act, wastes time thinking too much, isolated, doesn't work well with others

Learner: A know-it-all, lacks focus on results, learns a lot—produces little, bookish

Maximizer: Perfectionist, picky, never good enough, always reworking

Positivity: Insincere, naïve, superficial, Pollyanna

Relator: Lives in a clique, has an inner circle, plays favorites, too slow to warm to newcomers

Responsibility: Micro-manager, obsessive, can't say "no," take on more than you can chew

Restorative: Focuses on weakness, punitive, negative, critical

Self-Assurance:	Arrogant, self-righteous, over-confident, stubborn
Significance:	Recognition hungry, self-focused, needy
Strategic:	Jumps to quick decisions, difficult to understand their thinking, provides too many options
WOO:	Fake, shallow, does not care about deep relationships

QUESTIONNAIRE: CORRECTING OVERUSE

- How and when do you overuse your Strengths?

- What actions will you take?

- How can the team best support your effort to minimize your overuse?

STRENGTHS MATRIX

The goal of the Strengths Matrix is for everyone on the team to live your work lives above the horizontal line.

Step One: List the tasks, activities and assignments that comprise your job. Be as comprehensive as possible.

Step Two: Categorize each of these into one of the four quadrants.

Step Three: Work with your team to determine if you can trade anything that you have listed in the Learned Activities or Weakness boxes. These may be things your colleagues see as Strengths or Possible Strengths.

Step Four: Can you take any of their Learned Activities or Weaknesses, which might be a Strength or Possible Strength for you?

Note: This activity and more context around it can be found in Chapter 6.

STRENGTHS (GREAT AT/LOVE IT)	POSSIBLE STRENGTHS (NOT GOOD AT YET/ENJOY IT)
LEARNED ACTIVITIES (GOOD AT/DON'T ENJOY IT)	WEAKNESSES (NOT GOOD AT/DON'T ENJOY IT)

1:1 COACHING GUIDE

MONTHLY 1:1 COACHING GUIDE

Use these questions during your meetings. Sprinkle in questions over the course of many meetings. Don't try to cover all of them in one or two meetings.

Note: This activity and more context around it can be found in Chapter 6.

TALENTS AND STRENGTHS:

* Where can you link successes to the use of your talent themes?

* How can we optimize the use of your strengths?

* Is there one strength that you'd like to utilize more often? How can we make that a reality?

* How can I use my talent themes to best support you?

* Do you feel like you're positioned to excel?

* Do you still feel like your goals are well-suited to your talents and strengths?

EXPECTATIONS:

* What do you expect from me?

* What do you think I expect of you? How can we measure these expectations?

* Is there a performance goal we need to focus on over the next three months?

- How can we ensure your strengths are aligned with these expectations?

- Are there any goals you feel in danger of not achieving?

MOTIVATION:

- What is the most meaningful piece of recognition you've ever received?

- When you do outstanding work, what is the best way for me to recognize you?

- How do you like to be recognized? (Face to face? In writing? In front of others? Privately? More frequency?)

- When you achieve your goals, who do you want to know about it? Who inside the company? Is there anyone outside the company?

- What motivates you to do your job?

- What is the most effective way for me to motivate you?

DEVELOPMENT OPPORTUNITIES:

- Is there a skill or knowledge you'd like to learn? How can you gain that skill or knowledge?

- Is there a possible strength you'd like to practice to determine if it can become a strength?

- Is there someone in the company you'd like to learn something from? How can we measure your progress?

- What one thing, if you learned it, would make the greatest impact on your performance?

ONE-HOUR TEAM MEETING AGENDA

Note: This tool and more context around it can be found in Chapter 6.

- Behavioral Expectations Story: What examples can we share about our team or others in the company who have lived our Behavioral Expectations?

- Organizational News: What is happening in the company that we should know about?

- Team Performance: Let's discuss how we are performing in pursuit of our goals.

- Offer of Support: Who on the team needs help?

- Support through the Company: Is there another team who is struggling with something where we might be able to lend a hand?

- Old Business: Are there any outstanding items we need to discuss?

- Schedule for the Week: Based on our discussion, who will do what by when?

Note: The meeting facilitator should always send a follow-up email with action items so those aren't forgotten. There can also be an agenda item to deepen relationships. That might look like this: What is your favorite movie? Why is it your favorite?

TEAMWORK ANALYSIS

MY GREATEST CONTRIBUTION TO THE TEAM IS:	THREE THINGS THAT WOULD MAKE MY WORK LIFE EASIER ARE:
MY UNTAPPED POTENTIAL IS:	MY BIGGEST WORRY IS:

Note: At the team meeting, I'd suggest using one question per meeting so you can spend some time deciding how to use the answers. Here are debriefing questions for each item that you can use if you need them. You'll notice that the second question refers to other teams. Your team can lead the way in supporting others in the company in meaningful ways. Don't miss the opportunity to be a difference maker in your company. That said, if it feels overwhelming to think about other teams, stay focused on your team for now.

GREATEST CONTRIBUTION

- How can we best leverage one another's contributions?

- Can we show our appreciation to other teams for their meaningful contributions?

MAKE MY LIFE EASIER

- How can we lessen each other's burden?

- As a team, how can we make the life of other teams easier?

UNTAPPED POTENTIAL

- How can we tap into each other's potential?

- Whose potential in the company do we see being underutilized, and is there anything we can do to help that person realize his potential?

BIGGEST WORRY

- How can we minimize your worry?

- What are others in the company worrying about? Is there anything we can do to alleviate their stress?

RATE ME

In advance of monthly one-on-one meetings with team members, make sure each person comes prepared with specific answers to these questions:

Note: This activity and more context around it can be found in Chapter 7.

- On a scale of one to five, with five being high, how would you rate me as your manager?

- If the rating is a five, ask, "What am I doing that makes you rate me that way?"

- If the rating is anything other than a five, ask, "What can I do to make it a five?"

- If you're uncomfortable asking this set of questions, here is an alternative question that's effective: What is one thing I can do to be a better leader for you?

Note: This set of questions will put the level of trust between you and each team member to the test. If people feel safe, they'll be honest; if not, they won't. After you've spoken to each team member, evaluate if everyone opened up or if only some did. This can be an indication that your relationships are uneven through the team. As people provide answers, avoid becoming defensive or explaining away what they are saying. Instead, listen to understand and ask clarifying questions. If you do this, your level of trust will be bolstered. For each person, develop a plan of action. That means settling on specific behaviors people want from you. For those who gave you a five, ask them to provide you with specific behaviors so you can continue to repeat those. Follow through on the action plan and check in to see how it is going. Ask this set of questions, at least twice a year.

RECOGNITION AND DEVELOPMENT QUESTIONS

These are additional questions you can use at your Monthly 1:1 Meetings.

Note: This activity and more context around it can be found in Chapter 8.

Recognition Questions:

- If you were me, how would you best recognize you?

- What kind of work do you deem recognition worthy?

- What was the worst piece of recognition you ever received? What made it the worst?

- Who was the manager, teacher or coach who gave you the recognition you enjoyed the most? What did s/he do?

- What kind of recognition makes you feel the best?

- What motivates you?

- What do you find inspirational about your work?

- If you were isolated on an island, besides people, what would you make sure you had with you that you couldn't live without?

Development Questions:

- Who are the mentors in your life?

- What did you learn from your mentors?

- How can I help you improve?

- What's your dream job look like? What do you need to get there?

- If money didn't matter, what would you do with your time?

- What do you want to master so you feel most proficient in your job?

- What one wish do you have for your development?

GREATER GOOD MINDSET: ASSESSMENT AND DEVELOPMENT TOOL

ASSESSMENT

If you think about the Greater Good Mindset on a continuum, it looks like this:

....

Self-Serving Actions   Actions for the Greater Good

After reading the following questions, please place an "x" where you feel you stand today.

Note: This activity and more context around it can be found in Chapter 9.

Here are some questions that you can use to gauge where you fall on the continuum:

- Do I sacrifice my own needs for the needs of the company?

- Do I make decisions that benefit departments besides my own?

- Do I support other departments even when it makes more work for mine?

- Do I balance the support for my team and defend other departments when my team is adversely impacted by their mistakes?

- Do I support decisions that are made by those above even when I disagree?

Note: I find leaders have difficulty answering yes to most of these questions most of the time. It comes back to pressure for goals and a heavy workload. Additionally, the need to feel like we're supporting our team plays a role. It can prove helpful to refer back to these questions at the end of every week to see if you can keep moving right along the continuum.

GREATER GOOD QUESTIONS FOR MEETINGS WITH YOUR LEADER AND OTHER HIGHER LEVEL MANAGERS

- What is one thing our team can do to have the greatest impact on the success of the company?

- What aren't we doing that we should start doing to make the company more successful?

- Beyond being supportive of the decision ourselves, how would you suggest we handle interactions where other employees question the decisions that are being made?

- In your opinion, what could we do better as a department?

- What do you see as our greatest strength as a team?

- What do you see as our greatest contribution to the organization?

- Where do you see our untapped potential as a team?

ACKNOWLEDGMENTS

Thanks to Ed and Jan Jackson and Ed and Peggy Patrick, the best friends anyone could have.

Special thanks to David Brehmer, Drew Kishbaugh, and Jay Murray for their belief and support.

Gratitude to the Scribe Media team, especially Kevin, Julie, Bailey, Barbara, and Jessica, for getting me to the finish line when it seemed miles away.

ABOUT THE AUTHOR

JOE BERTOTTO has more than three decades of experience helping leaders improve their workplace environments and increase team productivity in a way that helps people live better lives. Joe works internally as the chief culture officer at Vizo Financial Corporate Credit Union and consults externally with numerous organizations successfully using this approach. Joe was one of the first Gallup Certified-Strengths Performance Coaches, and he and his wife, Judy, are the first married couple in the world to be Gallup Certified-Strengths Coaches. They have two grown, adventurous, and supportive children, Alex and Melanie. Joe played baseball at Temple University and enjoys Philadelphia sports.

Made in the USA
Columbia, SC
10 December 2019

84634938R00152